British Economic Policy 1970-74

Two Views

A View from the Outside

'A Self-confessed Monetarist'...?

RALPH HARRIS

General Director, The Institute of Economic Affairs

115461

A View from the Inside

In Place of Strikes

BRENDON SEWILL

Special Assistant to the Chancellor of the Exchequer,
1970–74

Published by
THE INSTITUTE OF ECONOMIC AFFAIRS
1975

First published March 1975

© The Institute of Economic Affairs 1975

SBN 255 36068 - 1

Printed in Great Britain by
GIBBONS BARFORD WOLVERHAMPTON
Set in 'Monotype' Bembo

Contents

Preface

The theme of the *Hobart Paperbacks* (an extension of the *Hobart Papers*) is the relationship between economic ideas and application, in particular the circumstances which decide whether or not an idea will lead to action.

Why do some ideas like PAYE, or 'fine-tuning', or reverse income tax find political favour and others like the extension of anti-trust laws from industry to trade unions, or selective social benefits, or market pricing for government services fail? Is the failure due to administrative impracticability? to 'political impossibility'? to civil service opposition? to obstruction by vested interests? to ignorance among political leaders about public acceptability?

Economic historians will be especially intrigued by the fate of the economic ideas of the Government of 1970–74, because it seemed ready to inject new – even unorthodox – thinking into government policy. Economists also are interested, although it is arguable that they should proceed with their thinking and make its results known whether they are thought administratively practicable and 'politically possible' or not. The fallacies of 'political impossibility' were incisively analysed by Professor W. H. Hutt in Hobart Paperback No. 1 (1971). He argued that economists should submit their findings in two parts: in pure undiluted form to indicate the *best* that economics can teach, and in a *second-best* form diluted by political judgement of what politicians can implement. If it is proper for economists to take administrative or political feasibilities into account in second-best advice, the pre-requisite is to know the precise and relevant practicabilities and limitations. The difficulty here is that the information about them reaches the independent economist mainly through politicians and civil servants, who cannot be neutral in interpreting them.

The task of an independent Institute concerned with research and education in economic policy is to find economists who are both authoritative and independent; the dilemma is that those who know usually cannot speak, and those who can speak may not know. On government policy the sources used by the outside economist are official publications and statistics, which may be incomplete, or tendentious, or selective. The best available sources may be people who have recently left government: mostly defeated politicians or retired civil servants. Even their lips may be sealed by loyalties, hopes of preferment or the Official Secrets Act.

The economic policy of the period 1970-74 is of exceptional interest to economists since a new government acquired power with evidently new policies that seemed to represent a clean break with the past, not only with the governments of other parties but also of its own. Yet the new policies seemed to fade out after 1½ years and the Government was brought down after 3½ years. Two earlier *Paperbacks* have a bearing on this period. In Hobart Paperback No. 2, *Government and the Market Economy* (1971), the consistency of Government policy in the first year was examined by an economist from the outside, Mr Samuel Brittan. In Hobart Paperback No. 5, *Bureaucracy: Servant or Master?* (1973), an American academic economist who has been a public official in Washington, Professor W. A. Niskanen, analysed the influence on economic policy of the machinery of government; it carried commentaries by two former British Ministers, Mr Douglas (now Lord) Houghton on the Labour side, and Mr Nicholas Ridley on the Conservative side, and by two former civil servants, Professor Maurice Kogan, broadly in sympathy with Labour, and Mr Ian Senior, whose sympathies are Liberal.

Paperback No. 7, *British Economic Policy 1970-74*, began with an approach from Mr Brendon Sewill, who was a Special Assistant to the Chancellor of the Exchequer from 1970 to 1974.

Mr Sewill, who learned his economics at Cambridge and not surprisingly emerged as a Keynesian, which he says he remains, offered the Institute his interpretation of the efforts made by the 1970-74 Government and the difficulties and obstacles it encountered. Since very little informed discussion of the events of the period by a participant has been published so far, Mr Sewill's account seemed of especial interest in indicating how the obstacles were seen from the inside, how they were confronted, and the nature and quality of the advice offered to ministers, not least by the Treasury. Mr Sewill presented the Institute with the difficulty that he was thus different from the authors typically commissioned: both at a disadvantage since he must be expected to be partial and at an advantage since he was exceptionally informed and authoritative. The decisive consideration was whether his interpretation would shed light on the period and stimulate discussion among economists, with some hope that valuable lessons would be learned for the future.

The interest of economists in Mr Sewill's chronicle is that it raises many of the fundamental questions of economic diagnosis of and treatment for the *malaise* of the British economy as it has developed in the post-war years under the influence mainly of Keynes's macro-economics, but also of Beveridge's and of Titmus's welfare state thinking, which can be said to have influenced if not dominated governments of both parties. Mr Sewill's account comprises a clearly argued and conscientious effort to identify, and to offer insights into, the influences which together decided how far and in what form the economic ideas with which the Government of 1970-74 set out emerged into policy:
– the relationship between long-term objectives and day-to-day pressures and preoccupations;
– the relationship between political philosophy and government management;
– the role of civil servants as executors of and advisers on government policy and guardians of continuity;
– the role of organisations of industry and trade unions as spokesmen for employers and employees and the danger of corporate collusion;
– the effect of increased taxation in exerting a deflationary (Keypress and television;
– the effect of increased taxation in exerting a deflationary (Keynesian) pressure or an inflationary pressure when unions are strong;
– the capacity of government to manage the economy if it is directly involved in raising funds to finance half of it;
– the attitude of employees to 'social wages' and the relevance (or irrelevance) of 'social wages' in collective bargaining;
– the persistent difficulty of reducing total government expenditure so long as the universal welfare state is thought sacrosanct;
– the relative effectiveness of policies designed to induce the unions to abdicate their monopoly power or to remove it by law;
– the reaction of business men to tax and other incentives as induce-

ments to invest given the uncertainties of government duration and
the arbitrariness of political attitudes;

– not least, the relevance of macro-economic thinking as an aid to
government policy.

Since Mr Sewill's account of monetary and non-monetary factors
differed at some important points from the analyses of the course of
events in the late 1960s and early 1970s argued by authors of earlier
IEA studies, it was agreed to precede his chronicle with a survey of the
monetary context of the period so that students of economics and of
the economic history of the recent past might have two approaches, one
by an insider and one by an outsider, for comparison and contrast. The
monetary approach has been written by Mr Ralph Harris, General
Director of the IEA, who has tried to clarify the widespread misunderstanding of the nature and the timing of the effect on output, employment and prices of changes in the supply of money. He has discussed
how far the course of events after 1970 can be interpreted in the light
of this 'monetarist' analysis, and does not exonerate the unions.

Mr Sewill's competence and authority derive from his combination
of experience in political and public affairs. As Director of the Research
Department of the Party that was to form the 1970-74 Government,
he was at the centre of the process of policy formation under the future
Prime Minister; he attended all meetings of the Shadow Cabinet in the
antecedent years 1965-70; he was responsible for drafting the manifes-
toes of his Party at the 1966 and 1970 General Elections; and in 1970 he
was appointed Special Assistant to the Chancellor of the Exchequer as
a temporary civil servant, in which capacity he attended all important
Treasury meetings, had access to the Chancellor, to senior Treasury
officials and to all official papers at the centre of economic policy. He
acted as political adviser and confidant to the Chancellor as one of a
small number of senior advisers recruited to help ministers overcome
civil service inertia. One of his tasks was to help in the presentation
of government policy to win public acceptance for its measures.

Mr Sewill's account discusses the role of monetary policy but emerges
with the view that the first essential that must be accomplished by a
government of any party is to remove the power of the unions to
dominate the economy and the government by the threat of strikes.
Mr Harris emphasises the primacy of monetary policy; he argues there
is increasing recognition by economists that this is the dominant
influence on policy, but that it is under-estimated by the Treasury and

the 'semi-official' National Institute of Economic and Social Research, and other groups concerned with short-term macro-economic forecasting such as the Cambridge Policy Group.

It must be left to readers to judge where the emphasis should lie, and how far the desired policy in the late 1970s should comprise government action on the supply of money and on the power of the trade unions. It may be that the two views, although apparently distant from each other, suggest ingredients of a composite policy that is beginning to be accepted more widely, not only by economists of all schools of thought but also by politicians of all parties: that the power of the trade unions has been enhanced by inflation, largely the outcome of pressure on government by the unions. If so, means will have to found, by a government of the existing parties, or of a coalition, or of a new alignment, to tame the unions as an *imperium in imperio* that must bow to the sovereignty of Parliament as did the feudal barons, the landed gentry and big business. And it may be that the best solution will be that offered by the market: that the most civilised method is to buy out the unions' legal privileges and monopoly powers by a sizeable sum that will compensate them but reduce their powers to those of other agents in the economy that are subordinate to Parliament.

It remains to add the disclaimer that the Institute's Trustees, Directors and Advisers do not necessarily share the views or conclusions for policy argued in this *Paperback*.

February 1975   ARTHUR SELDON

A VIEW FROM THE OUTSIDE

'A Self-confessed Monetarist'...?

*A resumé of the monetary theory of inflation
and its application to Britain since 1969*

RALPH HARRIS

The Author

Born 1924, educated at Tottenham Grammar School and Queens' College, Cambridge. Lecturer in Political Economy at St. Andrews University, 1949-56. General Director of the Institute of Economic Affairs since 1957. Author (with Arthur Seldon) of *Hire Purchase in a Free Society, Advertising in a Free Society, Choice in Welfare*, etc. Secretary of Mont Pelerin Society and Wincott Foundation. Member of Political Economy Club. Council Member of University College, Buckingham. Lectures and writes widely on post-war policies and economic requirements of free society.

I. Money in Theory

Cause and effect?

An acknowledged weakness of economics as a social science is that alternative theories cannot be put directly to the test by laboratory experiments. In the physical sciences, the operation of a specific variable can be studied by isolating the effects of changing it whilst all other forces are held constant. In the social sciences many changes are operating simultaneously, with widely diffused ramifications, so that it is usually impossible to disentangle either cause or effect with confidence or precision. Hence the familiar need to qualify economic generalisation, for example about the effect of a change in price on the amount supplied or demanded, by the textbook legend: 'other things being equal'.

But even in the real world of perpetual movement, one change may so dominate the customary ebb and flow of events that its origin can be sought in an equally marked change of some causal factor. Such a dramatic development may be seen in the unprecedented escalation of the fall in the value of money between 1970 and 1974. From an annual rise in prices oscillating between 1 and 5 per cent until 1968, inflation started spurting in 1970 and (with a significant pause in 1972) reached more than 20 per cent[1] a year by 1974. Amid all the disruptive consequences for the British economy and society, might there be a compensating gleam of hope that economists can get nearer to agreement on the virus which causes this potentially lethal economic fever?

---

[1] The official price index understates the rate of inflation which would be higher in the absence of subsidies on selected foods and the products of nationalised industries.

If economists cannot conduct controlled laboratory experiments to test conflicting theories, might the period since 1970 provide the next best thing as a proving ground for alternative explanations of the cause of inflation? Is there, indeed, one cause or several? If several, are all of equal precedence or plausibility? Can we be satisfied with behaviourist-type explanations that attribute inflation to 'world influences', the 'weakness of democratic government' or, as some would seem to say, to autonomous increases in costs and prices?

To judge by the present state of the debate, the choice is between variants of trade union cost-push or of monetary demand-pull. But can trade unions cause inflation without the collusion of government policy? Or does government policy cause inflation as a result of pressures which trade unions exert on them? In that event, what do we mean by 'cause'? Should we not distinguish between a proximate and a primal cause? And if so, is the former any more than an effect of the latter?

Since advance in understanding – as in industry – comes from competition between contesting endeavours, we should welcome a sharpening of the debate rather than contrive to seek a compromise or 'consensus' acceptable to politicians. In recent years experience of inflation in most countries has revived discussion of the role of monetary policy in the management of national economies. It cannot be denied that an increasingly formidable body of professional economic opinion has identified itself with the 'monetarist' school of thought. At its simplest, the proposition is that an increase in the quantity of money will – other things being equal – be followed by a fall in its value, or in other words by a rise in the general level of prices. But were other things equal between 1970 and 1974? Certainly this period saw an exceptional increase in the money supply which was followed by an unprecedented rise in prices. But does *post hoc-propter hoc* put the issue of cause and effect beyond dispute?

This question will not be resolved by pejorative labelling of participants as 'self-confessed monetarists' or by damning their analysis as 'extreme', 'rigid', 'mechanistic'. If we are to get closer to the truth of the matter, it will be by an appeal to the evidence of experience. Since interest in this question extends far beyond economic theorists to thoughtful laymen, my aim is to present a simple exposition of the monetarist approach and its application to recent events in terms that non-economists can judge for themselves.

The leader and the lags

Although economists have debated the relationship between money and prices for centuries, the restatement in modern terms of Irving Fisher's classic Quantity Theory was set out by Professor Milton Friedman in a *Paper* published by the IEA shortly after Mr Edward Heath formed his administration in 1970.[1] For practical men who tend to scorn 'academic theory' (on which they unwittingly rely in running their businesses), it must be emphasised that Friedman's scholarly formulations claim support from extensive empirical evidence of inflations and deflations in many countries over hundreds of years.

His *Paper* listed 11 'key propositions of monetarism' which might be crudely summarised as warning politicians that inflation would inevitably follow from 'a more rapid increase in the quantity of money than in output'. But while the man described by journalists as the 'guru' of monetarism was perhaps dogmatic in asserting that 'inflation is always and everywhere a monetary phenomenon', he acknowledged that the link between changes in monetary supply and prices is more certain in direction than in magnitude. In other words, there is a positive correlation but it is complicated by feed-back effects and it is not a straight line, one-for-one relationship.

Above all, the leader of the monetarist school emphasised that the link is complicated by the time-lags between an increase in the quantity of money and the effect on (a) output and employment and (b) prices. To quote from his second key proposition:

'The relationship is not obvious to the naked eye largely because it takes time for changes in monetary growth to affect income and how long it takes is itself variable'.

From studies of national economies 'under widely different conditions', Friedman confessed to being 'astounded' at how regularly an 'average' delay of six to nine months occurred between a change in the rate of monetary growth and a change in the growth of output and employment. Since the effect on prices 'typically' follows six to nine months later, Friedman pointed out that the interval between monetary change and price effect 'averages something like 12 to 18 months', although the full adjustment might take several years to work itself through the economy.

---

[1] *The Counter-Revolution in Monetary Theory*, Occasional Paper 33, 1970 (3rd impression, 1974).

Deficits do the damage

In understanding recent experience, it is helpful to recall the mechanism by which an increase in money supply is brought about. Friedman's ninth 'key proposition' explained the matter simply:

'Government spending may or may not be inflationary. It clearly will be inflationary if it is financed by creating money, that is by printing currency or creating bank deposits. If it is financed by taxes or by borrowing from the public, the main effect is that the government spends the funds instead of the taxpayer or instead of the lender or instead of the person who would otherwise have borrowed the funds.'

Again, the mechanism is plain in principle though subject to variations in its operation. At its simplest, if the government runs a budget deficit which is not financed by genuine borrowing (i.e. from the non-bank, private sector), the result is to expand the volume of monetary demand in the economy. Depending on the extent of under-used capacity, output and employment would be expected to rise during the following year.

But growing output cannot be expected to match a continuing increase in demand. As the scope for 'growth' in goods and services exhausts itself, the higher level of demand runs into a more or less constant rate of output and tends to push prices upwards. The full effect on the price level, however, may be mitigated by a diversion of part of the swollen purchasing power to an increased demand for imports. The resulting deficit on the current balance of payments thereby offsets the budget deficit and reduces the immediate impact of increased demand on the rate of domestic inflation. Such a moderating influence is of course reversed when the time comes to service or repay the resulting foreign debts. Meanwhile, the extent to which increased domestic demand is met by an import surplus indicates the degree to which inflationary pressure is 'exported' to other national economies.

What about wages? . . .

A further preliminary word must be said on the more contentious issue of the part played by trade unions exercising monopoly power to enforce wage increases in excess of the value of labour productivity at current prices. An employer conceding such an increase may be in a strong enough position in the market for his goods to pass the increased cost on to his customers. Insofar as they have to pay the higher price, they will have less to spend elsewhere, thereby exerting a downward pressure on other prices. So long as monetary demand in total is not inflated, the result of such a shift in incomes and spending would be a change in *relative* prices but not in the *general level* of prices.

If a strong trade union extracts an increased wage from a company that cannot recoup the cost by raising its prices, the result, in the absence of monetary inflation, would be an increase in unemployment. In neither event can powerful unions enforce a rise in the general price level, unless monetary supply is inflated to ease the change in relative prices or to maintain total demand for products and labour at a higher level of prices.

. . . and commodity prices?

Something of the same analysis applies to the other contentious issue, the effect on domestic inflation of higher prices for imported commodities. If the cost of a product suddenly rises (due to reduced supply or increased demand), the effect in a market operating under stable monetary demand is that the resulting higher price can be paid only to the extent that less is spent on other goods and services. Thus the famous rise in the price of beef could not have contributed to a general, continuing inflation unless monetary expansion had enabled consumers to maintain their demand without sacrificing alternative lines of expenditure. In the absence of such a general domestic inflation, we would expect some change in *relative* prices, even after a measure of substitution for the more costly products.

Where the higher prices apply to imported products, as in 1972-73, there could however be a modified effect on the general price level as a result of the adverse shift in the terms of trade. Thus if British exports exchange for a reduced volume of imports, the result *in the absence of an increased trade deficit* would be a smaller total volume of goods on which British consumers could spend their purchasing power. In addition to changes in relative prices, there would thus be a *general* 'inflationary' effect due not to monetary expansion but to the *real* loss in average exchange value of the same stock of domestic money. The qualification in italics suggests why this alibi for domestic inflation can hardly be pleaded by the British Government since 1972.

By running an increased deficit on foreign trade, the British economy has enjoyed a larger net supply of goods over which domestic demand could spread itself. Inflation today would therefore be to that extent higher if imports were reduced to the level that could be financed from increased exports. At the same time, the cost of British imports was raised by the sharp fall in the exchange value of the pound which so far from causing inflation in Britain resulted from rising domestic prices.

II. The Real World: 1970-74

The Conservative Party came to power in June 1970 with a strategy that had been worked out under Mr Heath during the previous five years. Its emphasis was on the structural reform of trade unions, taxation, housing policy and membership of the EEC aimed to create a more dynamic economy. During the election campaign inflation had not been the dominant issue and Mr Heath always denied that the phrase about cutting prices 'at a stroke' had played any part in the campaign.

Restriction of incomes and prices . . .
The resulting paradox was that the Government Party, which by common agreement had prepared for office more thoroughly than any previous Opposition, was caught facing the wrong way. Its long-term strategy may have been well-devised; it certainly carried wide approval at the 1970 General Election, despite Mr Wilson's characterisation of 'Selsdon man'. But in government, confronted with prices rising at more than 6 per cent a year, ministers were not ready with tactical measures to deal with the resulting pressures and tensions. And in the end it was the central cancer of inflation which not only dominated events but disrupted the grand strategy and finally brought Mr Heath down in February 1974 resisting what he regarded as a breach in an incomes policy he had pledged to shun like the plague.

In the absence of a well-prepared policy to deal with the admittedly awkward combination of rising prices and mounting unemployment, the new Government was bit by bit driven to improvise measures which amounted to a fairly complete abandonment of its distinctive reforms of domestic economic institutions. Its Chancellor of the Exchequer, Mr Anthony Barber, certainly pressed ahead boldly with his programme to reform and reduce personal and company taxation. But in place of imposing stricter commercial sanctions on ailing companies and nationalised industries, the Government distributed subsidies on an unprecedented scale in a desperate bid to combat unemployment and force growth fast enough to overcome the pressure of inflation then running at around 8 per cent a year. After an effort to win trade union agreement for wage restraint, it reluctantly resorted to compulsory controls over prices and wages. Having abolished Labour's Prices and Incomes Board in its first fling after 1970, the Prime Minister in November 1972 personally launched a statutory standstill as the first phase of a full-blooded incomes and prices policy which led remorselessly to defeat in February 1974.

. . . Expansion of demand

In addition to rising prices, the Government was faced from the outset with a perversely rising trend of unemployment. By 1971 – in the midst of distractions over Ulster, a succession of disruptive strikes accompanied by violent picketing and the drama surrounding the bankruptcy of Rolls-Royce and Upper Clyde Shipbuilders – newspaper and broadcast headlines heralding the approach of 'a million on the dole' proved too much for harassed ministers.

Concern about the continued rise in the official unemployment figures was aggravated by earlier Treasury assurances that the trend would turn down early in 1971. In his evidence to the first Wilberforce inquiry into the power workers' dispute at the beginning of 1971, Sir Douglas Allen as Permanent Secretary to the Treasury left no room for doubt that the Treasury were completely confident – even complacent – about their ability to regulate short-term demand so as to control the level of unemployment. Instead, as Treasury optimism was increasingly contradicted by the mounting monthly figures through 1971, the Chancellor felt driven to resort to 'reflationary' measures by expanding government expenditure while reducing taxation. The result was a series of budget deficits which started at little over £1,000 million in 1971 and climbed to above £4,000 million in 1973-74. It is from this source that we can trace the increasingly rapid growth of the money supply. If we take the broad definition of M3 (defined in the note to Table I), which was admittedly boosted by the upsurge of bank lending following the replacement of credit control by competition in banking, the money stock grew by a staggering 60 per cent in two years.

Before turning to the central question of the efficacy of monetary policy, we can learn one clear negative lesson from the experience of the 1970-74 Government. The plain conclusion must be that, whatever the causes of inflation, the far-reaching controls over prices and incomes launched in November 1972, provided no remedy. Table I shows that in 1971-72 the quarterly rises in retail prices declined from an annual rate of 10 per cent to 6 per cent. By 1973 the pace had quickened again to 10 per cent, and in 1974 it rose towards 20 per cent.

On a monetarist calculation, the inflation inherited by the Labour Government in 1974 stems directly from the monetary excesses begun by Mr Barber in 1972 (Chart p. 18, Table I p. 19).

III. Money in Practice

Friedman's 1970 *Paper* offered a 'concluding caution' which might almost have been addressed directly to the newly-elected Conservative Government. After hammering away at the dominant influence of changes in the money supply on prices, output and employment, the international authority on 'monetarism' warned against the temptation of using this potent instrument for 'fine-tuning' the level of activity in the economy. He emphasised that there is no 'precise, rigid mechanical connection between money and incomes' and recommended adherence to the monetary rule of maintaining a steady 'month-in, month-out, year-in, year-out' rate of monetary growth in line with the underlying increase in real output.[1] Experience since 1970 lends added force to the merits of this modest aim:

> 'It will not produce perfect stability: it will not produce heaven on earth: but it can make an important contribution to a stable economic society'.

The famous U-turn
The newly-elected Government did not, of course, start from a stable position. The previous Labour Chancellor, Mr Roy Jenkins, had cut back the rate of growth in the money supply from well above 7.5 per cent in 1968 to some 3 per cent following his Budget in 1969.[2] Since

---

[1] Elsewhere Professor Friedman has argued that to move from a high rate of inflation towards stability, a *gradual* reduction in the rate of increase in monetary supply is desirable to diminish the transitory effects on the level of unemployment.

[2] In his Budget speech (15 April, 1969) Mr Jenkins, after acknowledging that the increase in credit had been excessive in 1968, concluded: 'We cannot allow credit to be supplied on anything like this scale in the coming year'.

prices were already moving upwards at 5 per cent a year and would continue to go higher (reflecting the earlier monetary expansion), the impact of so sharp a monetary squeeze was bound to be felt in a more or less simultaneous slackening of the growth in output and rise in unemployment through 1970 and into 1971. At the same time, in 1970 came a surge of earnings – with increases averaging well above 10 per cent a year – in the effort by trade unions to make up for the imagined sacrifices of Labour's successive incomes policies (whose prescribed 'norms' were always exceeded). In the new environment of severe monetary contraction, higher labour costs were bound to intensify its ultimate impact on rising unemployment.

Hence the dilemma facing the incoming Government between tackling the long-term inflationary hangover of the pre-1969 monetary expansion or trying to abate the more immediate impact of the 1969 monetary contraction on unemployment, made worse by the acceleration of earnings which had got strongly under way before the election in June 1970. After a brief effort to lean against excessive wage settlements (the N minus 1 formula), it seems clear that the failure of unemployment to turn down as quickly as the Treasury predicted led to the abandonment of the struggle.

So it came about that the Chancellor launched into a massive monetary expansion towards the end of 1971 – just when (as Tables I and II show) the rising trends of both prices and unemployment were on the turn as a result of previous monetary policies! In the Budget of 1972, when the improvement was still plainer to see, the Government decided to 'go for growth' by budgeting for a deficit of £3,000 million. Instead of soldiering on with moderate monetary policies, the Chancellor finally adopted a 5 per cent growth target which the *Economist*[1] had been urging in the months of rising unemployment. As though to prepare for the inflation to come, he decided shortly afterwards to abandon his commitment to fixed exchange rates by announcing that the pound would float (i.e. sink).[2] By the end of 1972 the rate of increase in M3 approached an unprecedented 30 per cent.

---

[1] The *Economist's* record on the money supply had been at best confused. After preaching a tighter grip on money supply throughout 1970, the rising unemployment caused it to shift in 1971 to advocacy of 'reflation' plus a statutory incomes policy.

[2] By the end of 1973 the pound was effectively devalued against leading currencies by about 20 per cent which accounted for some 5 per cent of the increase in domestic prices during the previous two years.

How much unemployment?

Lest this emphasis on the monetarist interpretation of events leading up to 1971 be thought to display too much wisdom after the event, sceptics might dwell on the prescient verdict of Mr Samuel Brittan on Mr Jenkin's last Budget. In the *Financial Times* (15 April, 1970), he drew attention to the likely results of incomes increasing about three times faster than the money supply:

' . . . if rapidly rising wages collide with a slowly moving money supply, something will have to give somewhere. Either unemployment will increase, and there will be larger incomes per head for fewer people, or the monetary guidelines will give way.'

The record leaves no room for doubt that it was monetary restraint which started to 'give way' about a year after the 1970 Election.

The reason for this fateful change of course was concern about the highly publicised figures of mounting unemployment throughout 1971. The Government might have resisted the stampede by pondering the reassuring press report of the latter-day Jarrow 'marchers' who joined a demonstration in London after travelling down comfortably by Pullman train. But in addition to misjudging the trend of unemployment, it made the further error of failing to grasp the deceptive nature of the official statistics as a measure of the absolute level of 'unemployment', let alone as a measure of social distress in an age of wage-related benefits and prompt tax repayments.

In an IEA *Monograph* with the pointed title *How Much Unemployment?*[1] Mr John Wood demonstrated that the headlines about 'a million on the dole' provided a completely false impression of the numbers that might be drawn into employment by the conventional Keynesian techniques of boosting expenditure via deficit financing. Impressive evidence for this judgement is provided by the failure of the massive increase in aggregate spending after 1971 to reduce the official statistics for unemployment below 500,000 in 1973 when the incomplete official measure of 'unfilled vacancies' exceeded 360,000. The famous 'million' is revealed as a largely phantom army when account is taken of people moving between jobs (contributing to the million job-changers every *month*), of the voluntarily unemployed, and of the frankly unemployable (including those officially described as 'somewhat unenthusiastic in their attitude to work').

---

[1] Research Monograph 28, IEA, 1972.

It is acknowledged by many economists outside the ranks of monetarists that a serious inflation cannot be stopped without some transitional cost in unemployment. One obvious reason is that more jobs and wages are based on the expectation that inflation will continue, thereby enabling employers to cover their costs by raising prices. As inflation is abated – whether by monetary or other policies – confounded expectations must lead to marginal shedding of labour that now appears expensive. But there is no foundation in monetary theory for the fear that the rise in unemployment need continue progressively to very high levels. Insofar as unemployment is aggravated by 'excessive' wage increases, trade unions will settle for more modest increases as monetary policy shows sign of reducing inflation as well as employment prospects.

Thus already in Britain today there are signs that if some trade unions moderate their wage demands it will owe more to the growing apprehension of short-time working and unemployment than to the unsubstantial 'fig-leaf' of the 'social contract'. As Friedman argues in a forthcoming IEA *Paper* on the 'Phillips Curve',[1] the inauguration of monetary stability requires the acceptance of a 'natural rate' of unemployment, which can be reduced without inflation only by structural changes to remove ignorance and restrictions and so improve the occupational and geographical mobility of the labour market. If this argument is correct, unemployment can be pushed below the 'natural rate' by increasing monetary demand only at the cost of prices escalating towards an explosive inflation. Hence the futility of setting a 'full employment' target above the level implied by this 'natural rate': it can be approached only by abandoning price stability and then not reached for long without increasing doses of monetary expansion.

How much inflation?

The pressure of rising unemployment figures, as magnified by their official presentation, was sharpened by prods and goads from the TUC, the CBI and the Labour Opposition which vied with one another in calling for 'reflationary' action.

In 1971 it would therefore have required a strong resolve for the Chancellor to resist the temptations of monetary expansion. To begin

---

[1] Milton Friedman, IEA Occasional Paper 44, 1975.

with, Treasury orthodoxy does not appear to have given high priority
to the money supply as an influence on the rate of inflation. Further-
more, if the budget deficit were to be financed by government borrowing rather than by monetary expansion there would follow a rise
in rates of interest which were being deliberately held down in the
hope of stimulating investment and economic growth.

In this period of hesitancy it is not difficult to guess that the balance
was tipped against monetary caution by the persistent calls for 'reflation'
from the National Institute of Economic and Social Research (NIESR).
Invariably described in the press as 'influential' and 'prestigious', the
NIESR publishes a quarterly *Economic Review* which presents its short-
term forecast of the course of the British economy and specifies the
policies thought necessary to correct the ups and downs in such macro-
concepts as employment, output, exports, investment. Its record was
examined in an IEA study[1] which revealed surprisingly large errors[2] in
its short-term forecasts leading to a 'persistently inflationary bias' in its
policy prescriptions. True to form, from 1970 onwards the NIESR
lent its 'semi-official' weight to 'reflationary' measures, and the Budgets
for 1971 and 1972 followed very closely its proposals for a stimulus
of £500 million and £2,500 million respectively.

An illustration of what some may judge a reckless support of inflationary policies was provided in its *Review* of February 1972, which
advocated a 'reflationary' stimulus of £2,500 million:

'We have to acknowledge our inability to predict with any confidence what the resultant effects on inflation would be. But we have
also to acknowledge that, so far as value-judgements go, we now
put the earliest possible reduction of unemployment very high in
relation to any risk of accelerating inflation some years hence.'

By May 1973, newspaper commentators unaided by the NIESR's
pretentious forecasting model were increasingly pointing to the danger
of 'over-heating' the economy as judged by sharply falling unemployment, rising unfilled vacancies, upward pressure on costs, mounting
deficits on foreign trade and the sinking of the floating pound. Yet the

---

[1] George Polanyi, *Short-term Forecasting: A case study*, Background Memorandum 4,
1973.

[2] It has been well said by a more successful private forecaster that if the NIESR (or
Treasury) had to live by selling their forecasts, they would have improved their methods
or gone out of business long ago.

NIESR – undeterred by having been £1,000 million on the wrong side in forecasting the 1972 current balance of payments – persisted with its expansionist hopes and complained that others were warning against 'over-heating the economy – often without being too precise about the meaning of the term'. In another classic misjudgement, the May 1973 *Review* concluded:

' . . . there is no reason why the present boom should either bust or have to be busted . . . '

If the dangerously fallible forecasts of the NIESR exercised undue influence over the course of economic policy in these critical years, the explanation is partly that both the National Institute and the Treasury appear to have adopted similar econometric models which under-play monetary and pricing relationships.[1] Their mutually reinforcing errors have no doubt been cemented by the periodic movements of senior staff between the Treasury and the NIESR whose work has been heavily subsidised from public funds. This unhelpful relationship explains why Mr Norman Lamont, MP, in calling for a Royal Commission on the Treasury's management of the economy, regretted that the NIESR provided no independent check on its forecasting methods.[2]

The lags and laggards

On a broad monetarist interpretation of this period, the key error that led the Government to yield to these pressures and unwittingly to sow the seeds of the present super-inflation appears to have been an elementary misunderstanding of the delayed-action time-fuse that operates in the monetary mechanism. Tables I, II and III (pp. 19-21) will enable the reader to trace the effect of changes in the money stock (M3) on subsequent movements in prices, unemployment, output and the current balance of payments. To assist further in a judgement between M1 and M3 as the best approximate guide to monetary expansion, Table IV (p. 22) shows the growth in the Budget deficit (or 'borrowing requirement') which Friedman identified as the gap through which increased money enters the system.

[*continued on p. 22*]

---

[1] Writing of the medium-term forecast of the Cambridge Economic Policy Group, which displays similar defects, Mr Samuel Brittan criticised 'the type of economics without money and without price which has flourished in this country in the past 30 years.' (*Financial Times*, 17 February, 1975.)

[2] *The Times*, 24 February, 1975.

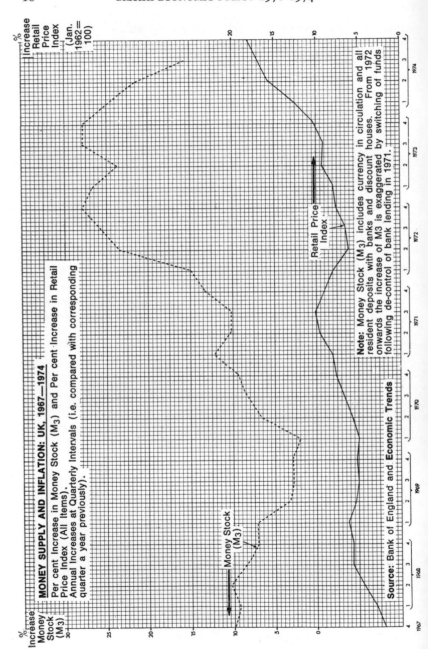

MONEY SUPPLY AND INFLATION: UK, 1967—1974

Per cent Increase in Money Stock (M₃) and Per cent Increase in Retail Price Index (All Items).

Annual Increases at Quarterly Intervals (i.e. compared with corresponding quarter a year previously).

% Increase Money Stock (M₃)

% Increase Retail Price Index (Jan. 1962 = 100)

Money Stock (M₃)

Retail Price Index

Note: Money Stock (M₃) includes currency in circulation and all resident deposits with banks and discount houses. From 1972 onwards the increase of M₃ is exaggerated by switching of funds following de-control of bank lending in 1971.

Source: Bank of England and Economic Trends.

TABLE 1
MONEY SUPPLY AND INFLATION, 1968-74
Per cent increase : Annual Rate[1]

	Money Stock M_3	Index of Retail Prices January 1962 = 100
1968	%	%
Quarter: 1	9.5	3.0
2	10.3	4.5
3	8.6	5.6
4	7.3	5.6
1969		
1	7.4	6.2
2	3.4 ⎫	5.4
3	3.0 ⎬ Monetary	5.0
4	3.0 ⎬ contraction	5.1
1970	⎪	
1	2.1 ⎭	5.0
2	6.9	5.8
3	8.5	6.9
4	9.5	7.7
1971		
1	12.4	8.1
2	10.4	9.8
3	10.4	10.1
4	13.4	9.2 ⎫
1972		⎪ Effect on prices due
1	15.0	8.0 ⎬ to 1969 monetary
2	23.6 ⎫ Monetary	6.2 ⎪ contraction
3	25.9 ⎬ expansion	6.5 ⎭
4	28.1 ⎭	7.7
1973		
1	26.9	8.0
2	23.9	9.3
3	28.1	9.2
4	28.0	10.3
1974		
1	24.9	12.9 ⎫ Effect on prices due
2	21.5	15.9 ⎬ to 1972 monetary
3	15.8	17.0 ⎪ expansion
4	n.a.	18.2 ⎭

[1] I.e. increase over same quarter of previous year.

Note: Money Stock M_3 includes currency in circulation and all resident deposits with banks and discount houses. From 1972 onwards the increase of M_3 is exaggerated by switching of funds following de-control of bank lending in 1971.

Source: Bank of England and *Economic Trends*.

TABLE II
OUTPUT, 'UNEMPLOYMENT', VACANCIES, 1968—74

	Output[1] GDP at Factor Cost 1970 prices % increase: annual rate[2]	Official 'Unemployment' (Excluding school-leavers and adult students) Monthly average seasonally corrected (No. 000)	% of total employees	Vacancies (GB) Monthly average seasonally corrected No. (000)
1968				
1	4.1	573.7	2.4	180.5
2	2.5	580.9	2.5	181.2
3	4.4	576.6	2.4	187.6
4	4.9	567.6	2.4	202.0
1969				
1	2.2	562.3	2.4	200.6
2	2.5	557.2	2.4	200.8
3	1.2	566.7	2.4	199.2
4	1.2	580.2	2.5	197.2
1970				
1	0.5	586.9	2.5	194.2
2	1.9	597.8	2.5	189.1
3	2.1	606.8	2.6	185.1
4	1.7	617.5	2.6	174.3
1971				
1	1.5	668.5	2.9	149.9
2	0.8	750.3	3.3	127.2
3	1.5	813.1	3.6	120.4
4	1.5	871.6	3.8	118.6
1972				
1	1.4	908.2	4.0	123.5
2	3.1	879.4	3.8	132.0
3	2.1	846.5	3.7	147.2
4	3.8	785.4	3.4	178.6
1973				
1	8.1	700.0	3.0	228.4
2	4.7	636.4	2.7	288.9
3	5.1	591.4	2.5	334.0
4	3.0	516.0	2.2	364.2
1974				
1	− 3.2[3]	570.1	2.5	285.1
2	0.4	579.5	2.5	309.2
3	0.9	629.0	2.7	306.0
4	− 0.8[4]	(735.4)[5]	(3.2)[5]	(196.3)[5]

[1] Average of expenditure, income and output-based estimates.

[2] I.e. compared with same quarter of previous year.

[3] 3-day week.

[4] Output-based.

[5] Figures for February 1975 (seasonally adjusted). Fourth quarter 1974 figures not published owing to industrial action by Ministry staff.

Source: *Economic Trends*.

TABLE III

BALANCE OF PAYMENTS, 1968-74
(current balance)

£ million
(seasonally corrected)

	Quarterly	Annual
1968		
I	— 94	
2	—102	
3	— 35	
4	— 49	—280
1969		
I	+ 19	
2	+ 96	
3	+164	
4	+170	+449
1970		
I	+252	
2	+135	
3	+ 80	
4	+218	+685
1971		
I	+135	
2	+284	
3	+385	
4	+246	+1,050
1972		
I	+ 84	
2	+121	
3	—110	
4	— 23	—72
1973		
I	—192	
2	—197	
3	—272	
4	—537	—1,198
1974		
I	—964	
2	—990	
3	—781	—2,735 (for three quarters)

Source: *Economic Trends.*

TABLE IV

BORROWING REQUIREMENT AND PUBLIC EXPENDITURE,
1970–71 to 1974–75
(£ million)

	Estimate	Provisional out-turn	Total public expenditure
1970–71	−244	617	22,000
1971–72	1,209	1,336	25,000
1972–73	3,116	2,118	28,500
1973–74	4,423	4,276	33,500
1974–75	6,331	n.a.	42,800

Source: Budget *Financial Statements;* 1974–75 estimates from the Supplementary *Financial Statement* following the November 1974 budget changes.

[continued from p. 17]

The Chart (p. 18) plotting changes in the money supply against the rate of price increases may be thought particularly illuminating. It shows that the rising trend of prices over this period was interrupted by a sharp fall from around 10 per cent in mid-1971 to about 6 per cent a year later. Turning to the trend of increases in the money supply we find an initial decline (from a high rate of increase around 10 per cent) starting in 1968 but falling below the ruling rate of inflation (around 5 per cent) in 1969. It is this interval of about two years which monetarists would claim relates the monetary squeeze of 1969 to the fall in prices of 1971. The corresponding link with output and employment may be discerned from a study of Table II. On Friedman's reckoning, we would expect the monetary contractions of 1969–70 to cause a slowdown in output and a rise in unemployment starting in 1970 and continuing into 1971, which is borne out dramatically by the figures presented in Table II.

The significance of this time-lag is that the Government intensified its monetary expansion in 1972 when the rise in unemployment was approaching its peak and could have been expected to fall anyway if the earlier more moderate monetary policy had been continued. But this sharp reversal serves a valuable scientific purpose by enabling us to judge the prediction from monetary theory that within a year output would increase sharply, and within two years prices would increase more rapidly. Thus the dramatic 'reflation' of 1972 can be shown to have spent its force in three directions: firstly, in pushing output up to reach a record rate of 8 per cent which could not be sustained (Table

II); secondly, in producing a deficit of more than £1,000 million on current balance of payments in 1973 (Table III); and finally, in propelling prices faster upwards in 1974.

Conclusive evidence that it was indeed these familiar time-lags which misled the Government is provided by a little-known exchange on this subject in November 1972. A group of independent economists sent Mr Heath a *Memorial to the Prime Minister* drawing attention to the inflationary consequence for the future of the already rapidly increasing monetary supply. His reply, which shows signs of having been drafted with the help of 'expert' advisers,[1] revealed a total unawareness of the time-lags familiar to first-year students of such matters. Declaring that 'our present inflation . . . can be said to have begun in effect in the autumn of 1969', he went on: 'This was a period in which central government was actually in surplus and the growth of money supply was unusually small.' Such an explicit misconception of the timing by which monetary policy must be judged did not prevent the Prime Minister concluding that 'a slowing down in the rate of growth of money supply is an essential part of our strategy' – this in November 1972, in the midst of a truly explosive increase in M3.

Supporting evidence for this central miscalculation was supplied by Mr Ian Gilmour, who with Mr Peter Walker has been among the most fierce critics of monetary policy as 'extreme' and 'rigid'. In a letter to *The Times* (6 January, 1975), he revealed himself as a laggard in comprehending monetary policy. He recalled the interval of tight money under Mr Jenkins in 1969-70 before asking:

'And what happened? Prices rose faster in 1969 than in 1968, and faster in 1970 than in 1969.'

As though to emphasise his own error in expecting an instantaneous impact, Mr Gilmour added:

'Despite the most rigorous application of the monetarist prescription, the disease got worse rather than better.'

With unconscious irony, Mr Gilmour concluded his dogmatic letter:

'I believe that dogmatism on this issue is still misplaced . . .'

---

[1] One of Mr Heath's Treasury Ministers, Mr Terence Higgins, was given special responsibility for supervising the money supply. Evidence that Mr Higgins also misunderstood the time-lags was provided by his contribution to an IEA Seminar on inflation in mid-1972 when he pointed to the slowing down of price increases to disarm criticism about the prevailing monetary expansion. A mild rebuke from Lord Robbins as chairman will be found on page 129 of *Inflation: Economy and Society*, IEA Readings No. 8, 1972.

Rival predictions

While the NIESR was calling for more 'reflation' and leading ministers were denying excessive monetary expansion, one of the leading British monetarists offered his prediction.[1] As early as June 1972, Professor Alan Walters condemned the 'explosive money supply' of which he said:

'. . . the implications are perfectly clear. The inflation will continue at a somewhat increasing rate – from the present five or six per cent to some 10 or even 15 per cent over the next year or two.'

A year later price increases verged on 10 per cent and within two years exceeded 15 per cent.

By 1973 the warnings were coming thick and fast, none more eloquent than from Mr Peter Jay. In May he wrote a prominent article in *The Times* (7 May) with the unambiguous title: 'The boom that must go bust'. It was a classic diagnosis of the acute stages of an inflationary fever that was still being fed by massive government expenditures, budget deficits and monetary incontinence. His impressive warning against the domestic over-heating and foreign indebtedness could hardly have been more alarming. Yet as late as November 1973, the Prime Minister stubbornly persisted with official optimism:

'. . . I believe that the prospects and opportunities for British industry today are more exciting and more solidly based than at any time since the Second World War'.[2]

Among the great and the good in whose company the Government erred were of course the official spokesmen for the CBI-TUC, whose pronouncements on this central issue could hardly be distinguished, and the leader-writer of the *Economist* who in September had rebuked 'those who have been talking Britain into an unnecessary panic' and told them sharply 'to listen'. His message was: 'Britain is two-thirds of the way to an economic miracle'.[3]

What about the unions?

Although Labour politicians in opposition were as uninhibited as the

---

[1] Joseph Sebag, *Newsletter* 4, 23 June, 1972.

[2] Speech to the Institute of Directors, reported in the *Financial Times*, 9 November, 1973.

[3] *Economist*, 1 September, 1973, p. 61.

NIESR or the *Economist* in urging 'reflation' on the Conservative Government in 1971, when it was still trying to combat inflation, Mr Denis Healey as Labour's Chancellor and one or two responsible trade union leaders like Mr Jack Jones have begun to echo the monetarist truism that excessive wage demands must increase unemployment in a régime of tighter monetary discipline such as the Labour Government is endeavouring to maintain. A fuller exposition of the remaining perils of Mr Healey's strategy, whereby a still more massive borrowing requirement is financed by running into debt overseas instead of resuming Mr Barber's domestic monetary expansion, will be found in *Crisis '75* . . . ?[1]

The aim of this brief survey is to test how far economic developments since 1970 conform to the yardstick provided by elementary monetary theory. Except in passing, I have not attempted to review alternative or supplementary explanations. An important disclaimer must, however, be added. 'Monetarist' economists – who are far from being the ideological sect of popular imagination – differ in their judgement on the part played by trade unions in 'causing' or aggravating inflation.[2] For my part, I have no doubt that a curb on the monopoly powers of trade unions would ease the harmonious operation of monetary policy, not least by reducing the cost in avoidable unemployment of establishing a stable economic and social order.

But even among those who put the primary blame on trade union 'pushfulness', it may be agreed that the Conservative Government's expansionist monetary policy immensely strengthened the effective power of trade unions (and others) to press for wage (and salary) increases without having to worry about the danger of unemployment which is now coming home to roost. If that lesson could be learned and taught by a Labour Government – which is certainly entitled to plead the present inflation as part of its appalling economic inheritance – the transitional discomforts of worsening inflation and unemployment that still lie ahead would be worth enduring. It may be acknowledged that Mr Heath's Government was beset with more than its share of ill-fortune, including a militant trade unionism that took the Industrial

---

[1] Occasional Paper Special (No. 43), IEA, 1975.

[2] A thorough discussion of this and related issues will be found in the proceedings of two seminars arranged by the IEA: *Inflation: Economy and Society*, 1972; and *Inflation: Causes, Consequences, Cures*, 1974.

Relations Act as a pretext for venting its political hostility to other policies. Amidst so many unpredictable difficulties and uncertainties, we may nevertheless judge the Treasury all the more culpable for failing to grasp the predictable cautions on inflation that standard monetary orthodoxy could have taught them.

To conclude on a hopeful note that may encourage British politicians in Government and Opposition to persevere with Friedman's golden rule of moderate, steady monetary expansion, I commend his verdict on its implications for the prized goal of economic growth.

'Steady monetary growth would provide a monetary climate favourable to the effective operation of those basic forces of enterprise, ingenuity, invention, hard work and thrift that are the true springs of economic growth. That is the most we can ask from monetary policy at our present state of knowledge. But that much – and it is a great deal – is clearly within our reach.'[1]

---

[1] Reproduced in Professor Friedman's article, 'The Case for a Monetary Rule', *Newsweek*, 7 November, 1972.

A VIEW FROM THE INSIDE

In Place of Strikes

BRENDON SEWILL

The Author

Born 1929. Educated Bryanston School. Read Economics, Cambridge. Joined Conservative Research Department 1952. Director of Conservative Research Department, January 1965 to October 1970. Special Assistant to Chancellor of the Exchequer, September 1970 to March 1974. National Executive Member, British Trust for Conservation Volunteers.

I. The 1970 Strategy

When many predict that the British economy, perhaps even British democracy, is on the verge of collapse, any attempt to look back to the comparatively calm days of the early 1970s may seem escapist. Yet there are lessons to be learned from experience.

As Director of the Conservative Research Department from January 1965 to October 1970, and then as Special Assistant to the Chancellor of the Exchequer until March 1974, I was in a good position to know the intentions of the Conservative Government which took office in June 1970, and then to see from inside the civil service the effect of the pressures of office and of events. Any eye witness account is inevitably liable to be partial (in both senses). I have, however, tried to avoid party politics. This is not written as a defence of the record of the Conservative Government, nor in any way on behalf of the then Chancellor of the Exchequer, Anthony Barber. Indeed I have concentrated more on the failures than on the successes. Nor does this comparatively short account set out to provide a full assessment of the 1970–74 record; that must wait until the events fall into perspective, the leading personalities complete their memoirs and the Cabinet papers are made public.

Nevertheless some preliminary and personal reflections may be of value both in recalling how we arrived at the present economic impasse and in suggesting how we should get out of it.

The purpose
The Conservative Administration of June 1970 was unusual in that it had a clear idea of how it wished to change society and a precise strategy for implementing the necessary policies.

Our analysis of Britain in the 1960s was conventional and well known. The slow rate of economic growth compared to other European countries would not only make us relatively poor but would also progressively tend to intensify the problems of sluggish management and restrictive labour attitudes. Frustration at the slow growth of living standards would mean a constant pressure for higher wages, thus making inflation harder to control. Moreover slow growth would tend to aggravate all the social problems of poor housing and education, deprivation, racial tension, violence and crime.

No-one was so naive as to believe the once fashionable theory that economic progress could be accelerated merely by increasing the pressure of demand. Something far more fundamental was required. The strategy was no less than an attempt to change the whole attitude of mind of the British people: to create a more dynamic, thrusting, 'go-getting' economy on the American or German model; to create not merely new material wealth but also a new pride in achievement. How long ago it all seems!

The programme
The main planks of the programme, in their pristine glory, were:

First, entry into the EEC to create a new challenge to industrial management, a new scale of operations and a new inspiration.

Second, the reduction, reform and simplification of taxation to create new incentives.

Third, legislation on industrial relations to create strong (yes, strong) but responsible unions.

Lesser planks were the change from agricultural subsidies to levies (which in the event was totally obscured by the rise in world prices), and the housing policy. The aim of attaching housing subsidies to families instead of to houses was partly to direct aid to those in need, partly to economise in public expenditure, but also realisation that the subsidised council house was a serious impediment to labour mobility.

The 'lame-duck' philosophy – that inefficient firms should be allowed to go bust – had a comparatively small place in our thinking in Opposition, was never mentioned at Selsdon Park, and achieved headlines only with Mr John Davies's speech in October 1970. Similarly, I recall no support among the pre-1970 Shadow Cabinet for *laissez-faire* proposals to abolish policies for regional employment and agricultural support.

Economic liberalism
Nevertheless the programme was one of economic liberalism, and it

was nearer to success than is easy to envisage in present circumstances. If the Conservatives had won the February 1974 election British membership of the EEC would have been firmly established, and the chances would have been that, given suitable amendments, the unions would have accepted the Industrial Relations Act.

Yet it is still a fair presumption that it would have taken a good deal more than that to alter the British way of life.

It was widely said that the Conservative Government took office in 1970 with a programme worked out in more detail than attempted by any previous Opposition. I make no apology for that. If a Party wishes to make fundamental changes in society, and to do so in time for the advantages to become apparent before the next election, it is essential for incoming Ministers not only to know clearly what they want to do, but also to have it worked out in sufficient detail to enable them to give confident replies to the initial queries of the civil service.[1]

A criticism which has more substance is that the strategic aim was decided too early. The narrow Parliamentary majority of 1964-66 lent urgency to an early policy review, and almost the complete pattern of policies was established by October 1965. This meant that by 1968 and 1969, when I proposed that price stability should be made the main priority, the mould had set too hard for any fundamental change.

I agree with those who now criticise the strategy as too materialist – too much efficiency and not enough idealism or principle. But at the time the analysis was widely shared, and there were many who saw in the creation of new prosperity the means of achieving not only social and environmental improvement but also a revival of national purpose and self-confidence. This aim was not ignoble.

It is also true that the members of the new 1970 Cabinet shared an impatience with the political compromises and shilly-shallying which were thought to have characterised the previous decade. There was a desire to take whatever decisive action was necessary – regardless of short-run political considerations – in order to drag the nation squealing and kicking into the new age. If it had succeeded, this approach would

---

[1] For the inter-action of incoming Ministers and the Civil Service, Richard Rose, *The Problem of Party Government*, 1974. He also discusses the role of outside advisers. Also Barbara Castle, 'Mandarin Power', *Sunday Times*, 10 June 1973; Marcia Williams, *Inside Number 10*, 1972; and Richard Crossman Diaries (to be published by Hamish Hamilton and Jonathan Cape), *Sunday Times* serialisation, 1975.

have been widely commended. In the event, however, an abrasive image was projected and antagonisms built up, so that in the end when an appeal had to be made to the people the necessary public support was not forthcoming.

II. Policies into Practice

Britain's EEC entry was undoubtedly the prime achievement of Mr Edward Heath and his Government. We had always foreseen that it would be controversial (indeed I had long hoped that the controversy might break up the class orientation of the two main political parties). What we had not foreseen was that the issue would not be settled outright. So instead of inspiration there was dispute; instead of new confidence, continued and damaging uncertainty.

The aim of the Industrial Relations Act was not to reduce the power of the unions, nor to blunt the strike weapon. Some legal protection was removed for certain types of unofficial strike, but nothing was done to reduce the force of official strikes. Indeed, the 'right to strike' was positively expressed in legislation for the first time in history. The Act set out to establish a legal framework for industrial relations (as exists in other countries) in the belief that it would lead to a gradual trans-formation of the unions into responsible and constructive institutions.[1]

It was recognised that there would still be tough bouts of wage bargaining (probably only every two or three years on the American pattern), but it was hoped that between whiles the reconstituted unions would collaborate in raising productivity and preventing unnecessary disputes. Thus progress could be made towards the goal of a high-wage/low-cost economy.

In Opposition, private talks with trade union leaders had led us to believe that, while the unions would be bound publicly to oppose the introduction of legislation on industrial relations, once the law was

---

[1] There is a mountain of literature on trade union law in general, and the Industrial Relations Act in particular, but for a short summary, C. G. Hanson, *Trade Unions: A Century of Privilege?*, Occasional Paper 38, IEA, 1973.

passed it would be accepted. Where we (and probably they also) went wrong was in not realising that such a head of opposition would be built up that it would become impossible for the law to operate properly. As with the EEC, we also miscalculated in assuming that Labour in opposition would maintain the policies they had initiated in government.

Reduction and reform of taxation

The third part of the strategy was the reduction and reform of taxation. The Chancellor's repute rose rapidly when he unfolded measure after measure in successive Budgets to fulfil to the letter all the tax pledges of the 1970 manifesto: the simplification and reduction of income tax, the abolition of a separate surtax, the replacement of SET and purchase tax by a buoyant and uniform VAT, the reform and reduction of corporation tax (although the main purpose here has been obscured by dividend control), free depreciation, the simplification of estate duty and capital gains tax, the overdue winding-up of the post-war credits, and the proposals for the tax credit scheme – the most advanced reverse ('negative') income tax scheme envisaged in any country.[1]

Much could be written on the pros and cons of all these changes, but here the central question is how far we succeeded in producing the incentives necessary to create a more dynamic economy. It is an ugly fact that incentives can only be improved by making the rich richer. This was the first time since full universal suffrage that any Government had espoused such an undemocratic (using Plato's definition of democracy as a state in which the poor plunder the rich)[2] process as its deliberate strategy.

Taxation as a proportion of GNP was reduced from 32 per cent in 1970 to 26 per cent in 1973 (if insurance contributions are included from 38 per cent to 32 per cent). The top rate of tax on earned income was reduced from 91 to 75 per cent. More important, the effect of the income tax simplification and reduction was to cut the apparent standard rate of income tax from 8s 3d in the £ (to the working man: 'nearly half') to 30 per cent ('less than a third').

---

[1] The details of the various tax reforms are set out factually in *The New British System of Taxation*, Central Office of Information, 1973.

[2] The full quotation from Plato is 'Democracy is a state in which the poor, gaining the upper hand, kill some and banish others, and then divide the offices among the remaining citizens equally'. (*The Republic*, Book VIII.)

It was noticeable that in each case when a completely new and – one hoped – rational tax scale was produced it was impossible to concentrate debate on the merits or demerits of the new scale. Parliament, press and public were interested only in how much was being 'given away'. Yet this could equally well be regarded as a measure of over-taxation in the past. This was another example of the characteristic emphasised by many observers that the British are more interested in the preservation of the *status quo* than in progress, more concerned with 'fairness' than with incentive.

Fairness and failure

Indeed, during the later stages of incomes policy 'fairness' became the watchword. The limits placed on salary increases counteracted the effects of the tax reductions. More recently the present Government has raised tax rates, and the gathering pace of inflation is sweeping the upper-income groups into higher and higher tax brackets. For the majority of wage-earners it probably remains true that taxation is less of a disincentive than in the late 1960s. In all walks of life, however, many have learnt that it pays better to take industrial action (that typically British euphemism for non-action) than to work hard and seek promotion. Inflation makes a nonsense of incentives – as of so much else.

The new ambitious attitudes of mind envisaged before 1970 were not created either by the tax changes, or by entry into Europe, least of all by the ill-fated Industrial Relations Act. The statistics show that over the period as a whole there was no noticeable increase in the rate of economic growth. For a variety of reasons the strategy failed: because Europe was oversold; because of the historically negative and distrustful attitude of British trade unions (accentuated by the move towards extremism of the past decade); because of the onrush of inflation, both home produced and imported; not least, because the British people (and who can blame them) preferred a quiet life.

It was a brave attempt. History may well record it as the last chance to avert Britain's often-predicted genteel decline to one of the poorest nations of Europe.

III. Monetary Policy

Governments are judged not only by how far they succeed in their stated objectives but also by how well they cope with the day-to-day running of affairs. One of the main criticisms of Conservative economic management has been that the money supply was allowed to expand too fast, thus creating the 1974-5 inflation. There is obviously an element of truth here but it would be a grave error to conclude that this was the sole or even the main cause of current economic troubles.

At the Treasury the orthodox view was that while the money supply had an important role, it was not the prime determinant of the rate of inflation. Thus the correct stance was that the monetary reins should be kept taut but no more. That is to say, the rate of growth of the money supply should be slightly less than the combined rate of growth of gross national product plus the current rate of inflation. To give a more savage tug on the reins would stop all forward progress of the economy. A restriction of the money supply could be achieved, directly or indirectly, only through a rise in interest rates, and that would mean less investment, less housebuilding, and a slower rate of economic growth. Applied more severely the result would be a liquidity crisis, widespread bankruptcies and a collapse of industrial confidence. There was no way in which monetary policy could be made to apply to inflation but not to the level of economic activity.

I did not dissent from that view at the time, and do not now. The Table shows that, so far as M1 is concerned, we did succeed in keeping pretty close to those guidelines. As the M1 definition of the money supply is 'coin and notes in circulation plus bank deposits on current account' there is literally no truth in the allegation that the Bank of England printing presses worked overtime. Indeed, it is worth noting

GROWTH, PRICES, AND MONEY SUPPLY,
1969-70 TO 1972-73

Period[1]	Rise in GDP[2]	Rise in Prices[3]	Growth + Prices[4]	Money Supply[5]	
				M1	M3
	%	%	%	%	%
1969-70	1.8	7.4	9.3	8.9	8.5
1970-71	1.6	9.4	11.2	12.9	10.4
1971-72	3.3	7.9	11.5	16.5	25.9
1972-73	4.8	9.9	15.2	7.8	28.1

[1] The period from 3rd quarter to 3rd quarter is used as this gives the fullest picture of the controversial year 1973, while avoiding the final quarter which was affected by the oil shortage and coal dispute.

[2] Growth of domestic product seasonally adjusted and at constant prices.

[3] All Items Index of Retail Prices.

[4] This of course is approximately equal to the rise in money GDP.

[5] Seasonally adjusted end-3rd quarter to end-3rd quarter.

that in the controversial years 1972-73 M1 increased less fast in Britain than in almost all other European countries.

Credit competition

The introduction of the new system of credit control in September 1971[1] for a time made the practical task of monitoring and controlling the money supply much harder. The change was necessary because the previous system of quota controls on bank advances was in danger of breaking down.

One view at the time was that the expanding role of the banks and the growth of the secondary banks was an inevitable, and on the whole desirable, consequence of more liberal policies. On this interpretation part of the growth of M3 during the two years following September 1971 was due to the change in the system and this would not have an inflationary effect. More recently, with the malaise of the secondary banks, opinion has tended to view their development as over-stimulated by easy money, and to suggest that competition for credit could work only if accompanied by a rise in interest rates.

[1] *Competition and Credit Control*, Bank of England discussion paper, May 1971.

Probably the truth lies somewhere between the two views. Even to the extent that the latter is correct, it does not prove that the growth in M3 directly affected the price level. It did undoubtedly, however, permit the boom in share and property prices which had an indirect effect on pay negotiations.

Another complicating factor is that in 1972 interest rates on bank loans were lower than those on certificates of deposit. This led to very large arbitrage operations. They had no inflationary effect, but were nevertheless reflected in an apparent increase in M3.

So for these reasons it can be held that during 1972 and 1973 M3 was not a reliable statistical indicator of the growth in the money supply. M1 was probably as reliable, if not more reliable, than M3. Those who quote only M3 to prove their case are in danger of being misled.

During the early 1970s all the countries of the Western world suffered from an excessive rise in the world money supply. From 1968 to 1973 the total of world reserves plus Euro-currency deposits trebled. But again, even if it is true that a flood of money leads to inflation, the converse does not follow: a drastic cut back in world money supply would not stop world inflation until it had first led to a reduction in economic activity and a rise in unemployment.

Monetary control alone?

This is not the place to go over the argument that has raged for the past decade between the 'monetarists' led by Professor Milton Friedman and those economists who believe that the main cause of inflation has been the cost-push monopoly bargaining power of the trade unions.[1] The important point is that now both schools seem to be coming much closer together. The monetarists now accept that, even with a fixed money supply, trade unions can force up pay and so put either their own members or others out of work; they maintain that it is governments which cause inflation by increasing the money supply to counteract that rise in unemployment. This of course is virtually the same as everyone else has been saying – that given a commitment to full employment, it is the monopoly power of the unions which forces up pay and prices.

---

[1] The latest state of play is set out clearly in *Inflation: Causes, Consequences, Cures*, IEA Readings No. 14, 1974.

No-one denies (and nor did they in the past) that if price stability is to be achieved, strict control of the money supply is one of the essential factors. Few would dissent from Professor Friedman's formula that once price stability is achieved, the money supply should ideally increase by about 3-5 per cent a year. The remaining difference is whether it would be more practicable, and cause less misery, to attempt to stop inflation by using monetary policy *alone*, or whether it might be better *also* to tackle the element of monopoly. It is curious that many academics who delight in criticising the politicians and civil servants for conforming to the 'politically possible' themselves fall into the trap of tacitly assuming that the obvious course of action suggested by liberal economic theory – reducing the monopoly power – is not 'politically possible' and instead fasten on the ineffectiveness of attempts to control it through varieties of incomes policy. But of that problem more anon.

What Professor Friedman and other advocates of a purely monetary solution to inflation have never been able to explain is how in the real world a strict control of the money supply would stop the use of the strike weapon by powerful groups successively to force up pay and prices.

Some economists argue that only a minority of unions have sufficient monopoly power, and that therefore all that is needed is a once-and-for-all adjustment of relative pay levels. But experience shows that it is a majority of unions which have the power – not only the coal-miners, but also the bakers, the seamen, the dockers, the power workers, the power station engineers, the train drivers, civil servants, the nurses, the doctors, the consultants, the North Sea oil drillers, the water supply workers, the sewage workers, etc. Many other groups have sufficient power to gain pay increases by threatening to force private firms into bankruptcy. The more it is proved that force pays, the more groups get organised to coerce the public. Moreover, there is absolutely no reason to see why the process should be once-and-for-all. Even with a stricter control of money the pay demands are likely to come in every year, if not more frequently. Professor Friedman himself admits that, if on a wide scale workers insist on demands which add up to more than 100 per cent of real income, ' . . . I see no ultimate outcome other than either runaway inflation or an authoritarian society ruled by force'.[1]

---

[1] *Monetary Correction*, Occasional Paper 41, IEA, 1974, p. 32.

How much unemployment?

The only way monetary policy alone could stop inflation is by creating so much unemployment that the unions were brought to their knees. It has never been tried, so no-one knows how much unemployment, how many bankruptcies, would be necessary. But the impression I gained in 1971-72 when unemployment reached its post-war peak was that, if anything, this situation led to a hardening of union attitudes rather than the reverse. In pre-war days unemployment did affect union strength because some men who were desperate for work were prepared to act as strike breakers. But one suspects that monetary policy would have to be very strict for a very long time before we returned to that situation.

We are left with two further propositions. First, that the rise in unemployment need only be temporary: this appears to follow from the (false) premise that only a once-and-for-all adjustment of relative pay is necessary. Second, and somewhat surprisingly, that the dislocation would be less if the monetary screws were tightened gradually and less harshly than has been the case since July 1973: but when one has seen the pressure on a Government to relieve unemployment (as in 1971-72) or to prevent a total collapse of industrial confidence (as in the autumn of 1974) it is difficult to believe that any Government could have the strength of will to maintain such a policy through a whole series of years in which unemployment remorsely rose and the national income steadily declined. In any event, in a democratic country it is not practical economics to advocate a policy which would be so unpopular as to lead inevitably to electoral defeat and reversal by the incoming administration. And the trouble about the monetary solution is that when in due course interest rates were reduced, full employment restored and growth resumed, we would be back to a situation in which unions would force up pay and prices just as at present.

While not pretending that everything in the past was perfect, one cannot escape the conclusion that if we were to rely on monetary policy alone, only permanent depression could keep inflation at bay. If the inescapable result of such a policy were permanent mass unemployment, it would be clear to all and sundry that the capitalist democratic system had failed. The conditions would be ripe in theory – and on the ground – for seeing whether a totalitarian or communist system could provide stability with less misery.

IV. Government Expenditure and Demand Management

The Ministers who took office in June 1970 were united in their eagerness to cut public expenditure. It was essential to wield the axe quickly before their ardour became cooled by Departmental responsibilities. In Opposition we had prepared a list of possible economies, and these formed the basis for action.

The results of the review were announced by the Chancellor in October.[1] They included *inter alia* the complete recasting of the housing subsidies and a phasing out of school meal and milk subsidies: total reduction £1,000 million by 1975. Even so, the forecast levels of public expenditure continued to rise year by year, although somewhat slower than the expected rise in gross national product.

A strict monetary and fiscal régime had been in force for the three years since devaluation in 1967. What few realised was how *slow* these policies would be to produce results – the improvement in the balance of payments to a current surplus of over £1,000 million in 1971, and the rise in unemployment which continued until the spring of 1972. Equally it was noticeable how slowly the economy responded when from March 1971 onwards the engines were put into reverse. The experience was akin to steering a super tanker through the Cowes regatta.

1971-72 recession
It was generally accepted that the correct Keynesian reaction to the rise in unemployment was to stimulate demand through the reduction

---

[1] For details of the public expenditure cuts, *New Policies on Public Spending*, Cmnd. 4515, HMSO, October 1970. Also Sir Samuel Goldman, *The Developing System of Public Expenditure: Management and Control*, HMSO, 1973.

of taxation. The October economies were balanced by a reduction of 6d in income tax. As soon as the trend became clear, substantial tax reductions were made in the 1971 Budget which was brought forward to March. This was followed by a further reduction of indirect taxation in July, but still unemployment rose inexorably.

An argument used by the monetary purists is that when, in the process of slowing down inflation, monetary policy starts to bite and produces unemployment, governments make the mistake of rushing to reverse it and that this was especially true of the Conservative Government in 1972. I would comment that by the spring of 1972 there was no evidence that inflation was being brought under control: on the contrary, with the success of the miners' strike it looked like getting out of hand. I will return to this point later (p. 49). What is true, however, is that governments always tend to over-react – the well-known phenomenon of too much too late.

It may well be that the unemployment statistics are misleading: what is undeniable is the pressure they create from Press, Parliament and Cabinet colleagues for further reflationary action. It is easy to say that Chancellors should resist such pressure and, if necessary, resign. But these issues are always ones not of principle but of judgement; resignation at a time of economic difficulty can be construed as un-patriotic in that it may shake industrial and foreign confidence. More-over, as the example of Mr Peter (now Lord) Thorneycroft (or earlier of Lord Randolph Churchill) showed, it only leaves in command those who are in favour of higher expenditure.

During the recession it became much harder to keep public expenditure in check. Treasury control of expenditure, however sophisticated the techniques such as PESC (Public Expenditure Survey Committee) and PAR (Programme Analysis and Review), depends ultimately on the Chancellor's strength and support in the Cabinet. Where there is any dispute between the Treasury and a spending Department the Treasury officials' only sanction is to threaten that in the last resort the matter will have to be taken to Cabinet. When it is obvious that there is a majority in the Cabinet in favour of increasing expenditure (as is likely when men and resources are lying idle) it becomes comparatively easy to call the Treasury bluff. Nevertheless public expenditure plans were deliberately tailored to increase during the recession and decline (as a proportion of the gross national product) during the following recovery.

Government expenditure and price stability
There can be little doubt that the higher the proportion of the national income represented by public expenditure and taxation, the harder it becomes to achieve growth and price stability. (At the extreme when 100 per cent of everyone's income is taken in taxation, and all goods and services are supplied free by the state, it is obvious that there would be no incentive for anyone to work, production would be almost nil and inflation – at any rate in the sense of excess demand – would approach infinity.) Yet in recent years it has not seemed that the main cause of inflation and slow growth has been either an unwillingness to work (except to the extent that strikes come under that heading), or an excessive level of demand. While public expenditure may have been an accessory before the fact, it has not been the leading inflationary criminal.

To be more specific, if a decision were now taken to reduce public expenditure from the present level of over 50 per cent of GNP to, say, 40 per cent with corresponding tax cuts, it would not diminish the pace of rising prices; if anything it would tend to cause an acceleration as the unions used their strength to fight for reimbursement for previously free or subsidised services.

Control of public expenditure, like control of the money supply, is important in the battle against inflation but not sufficient alone. Perhaps in the long run the only way to prevent the political pressures of democracy leading to a continual increase in public spending will be to have a written constitution protecting not only the basic freedoms but also containing entrenched clauses limiting the proportion of the national income to be consumed by public services.

Traditional monetary and fiscal regulation
I had for long been dissatisfied with the traditional methods of fiscal and monetary regulation. To cut taxes in a recession is easy enough, but there is always a tendency to delay an increase in taxes until a boom is seen to be well under way, when it is too late. An increase in taxation aggravates cost inflation. Similarly, any sharp increase in interest rates is liable to be interpreted by industry as the onset of the next 'stop' whereupon industrial confidence collapses, opening the way to the subsequent recession.

The Plowden Report[1] in 1961 drew attention to the disadvantages

---

[1] *Report on Control of Public Expenditure*, Cmnd. 1432, HMSO, July 1961.

of sudden starts or stops in public expenditure. Since then public expenditure had been out of fashion as a method of counteracting economic fluctuations. During the early 1970s, however, a new system for regulating public expenditure was being considered at the Treasury. This is best visualised like the animals going into the Ark. In normal times projects, having gone through the preliminary planning processes, advance to the starting line two by two. In a recession the rate is stepped up so they advance three by three; in a boom it is slowed down so they advance in single file. This provides considerable counter-cyclical leverage without undue disruption or inefficiency. But it is a system which can be applied only to part of public expenditure such as road building and construction projects; current expenditure on defence, education and health plod steadily on.

So in the winter of 1971-72 when it was clear that, in addition to speeding up expenditure, further action would have to be taken to stimulate consumer demand, it was desirable to find some method other than a reduction of taxation which would in due course have to be reversed. What was needed was a once-and-for-all injection of purchasing power. The repayment of all post-war credits, announced in December 1971, was one such measure. But it was not enough. One possibility which would be worth considering in similar circumstances in the future would be to make a single lump-sum 'capital' payment, perhaps of the order of £50 to £100, to each old-age pensioner. This would help to get us out of a recession without storing up trouble for the future, and would at the same time serve a valuable social purpose.

Unfortunately it did not prove possible to arrange such a scheme before the 1972 Budget, although somewhat surprisingly a stunted version did emerge nine months later as the £10 Christmas bonus. But of course by then the main purpose had passed by, and taxation had been substantially reduced.

An energetic and determined Minister can overcome almost all negative obstruction in his own Department. It is right to say we met practically none in the Treasury, partly because it is a small and high-calibre Department, partly because in seeking to keep down public expenditure and reform taxation we were working 'with the grain'. (The process proved much more difficult, for example, in the Department of Trade and Industry where Conservative Ministers were working against the whole interventionist purpose of the Department.) This does not, however, diminish the respect due to the Chancellor for his determination and mastery of detail in pressing through the tax and other reforms where previous Chancellors had failed. But it is difficult even for a determined Minister to overcome administrative blockages outside his own Department.

Treasury advice on growth

With the recovery from recession there seemed a real chance to get the economy on the path of sustained growth that had eluded Britain through so many stop-go cycles. The Treasury forecasts showed the possibility, without strain on the economy, of 5 per cent growth for some time, thereafter declining to a long-term rate of about 3½ per cent. Seeing the chance to secure the capital investment which had been so disappointingly low for so long, the Chancellor deliberately publicised the 5 per cent growth target. This was originally set for the period from the 1972 Budget to the first half of 1973, and then extended in the 1973 Budget for a further year. (It was, however, made clear that the rate of growth would tend to fall towards the end of this later period.)

Plugging this target laid him open to criticism that he belonged to the 'growth at all cost' school, but he felt it was more important to build up industrial confidence (and who, these days, can deny it?). Industry was desperately slow to get moving, but by the end of 1973 investment intentions were at a record level.

During 1973 there was a severe adverse movement in the terms of trade. The colossal rise in world prices added some £2,000 million to our import bill – even before the rise in oil prices. The question was whether to attempt to correct the balance-of-payments deficit by reducing the size of the public sector borrowing requirement (then running at about £4,000 million). This could have meant large increases in taxation or cuts in public expenditure. The general view was, however, that it would be wrong to slam on the brakes. With the hope that the rise in world prices might be temporary, with the advantage of the decision in 1972 to allow the pound to float, with the success (at that time) of the counter inflation policy, both the Treasury and many experts outside[1] felt – until the autumn of 1973 – that there was a reasonable chance that we might win through without another 'stop'.

---

[1] Including the NIESR, the CBI, TUC, etc.

There was also another consideration which became important towards the end of the year. To reduce the overseas deficit and the borrowing requirement inevitably meant holding down real incomes (that is, of course, the consequence of the adverse movement in the terms of trade). But to increase indirect taxation would have put up the price level: to have increased direct taxation would have cut pay packets. Either would have spelt the end of the statutory control of incomes. The resultant rise in pay would have been such as to maintain real incomes and render the policy ineffective.[1] The strength of the unions then, as now, was such that the Government were unable to take the necessary action.

Adherence to the 5 per cent growth target gave a superficial appearance that we were pressing on regardless. That was not so. I have already mentioned that public expenditure had been planned to decline as a proportion of the GNP. In May 1973 public expenditure was cut by a further £500 million. Calls for special deposits had been made in November and in December 1972, and in July 1973 monetary policy was tightened with a sharp rise in the minimum lending rate from $7\frac{1}{2}$ to $11\frac{1}{2}$ per cent. In December the Chancellor insisted on a further reduction of £1,200 million in public spending for 1974-75. Although easily forgotten as it was not enforced by the present Government, this was in real terms the biggest reduction in public expenditure ever announced and one of the most deflationary budgets ever introduced.

But by then the Arab-Israeli war had led to the cutback of oil supplies, and the coal-miners' dispute had begun. In early 1974 came the all-out coal strike, the 3-day week and the staggering rise in oil prices. Hopes of steady and sustainable economic growth which had glowed so brightly over the previous quarter of a century were extinguished.

---

[1] I.e. the situation projected by Professor Friedman, quoted on page 39.

V. Inflation

The wages explosion began in 1969, as a result of a variety of factors among which were the relaxation of the then Labour Government's prices and incomes policy, and the demonstration that the unions had the constitutional power to defeat the Government's proposals for trade union reform.

I was at that time concerned that the Conservative Party had no convincing policy to secure price stability. All the evidence coming across my desk was that the electorate desired price stability above all other political goals. Yet even then there was no meeting place between those senior members of the Party who believed that any interference in the working of market forces in the key area of pay and prices was doomed to fail, and those who, in an equally good liberal economic tradition, believed that the monopoly bargaining power of the unions meant that the free market could not operate unless the strength of organised labour was kept in check by some form of incomes policy.

'At a stroke'

In the somewhat desperate final days of the 1970 election a member of the Conservative Research Department produced a closely argued paper recommending, *inter alia*, an immediate reduction in indirect taxation and nationalised industry prices which would 'at a stroke' reduce the rise in prices. This paper was seen by the late Iain Macleod; in the confusion of the campaign it got issued under the name of the leader of the Party; it was hardly reported in the press; it had no influence on the result; it was never taken on board either by Macleod or by the rest of the incoming Cabinet; and it was only implemented by degrees. All of this was a pity as it would have been the right policy to pursue. It would have helped to avoid the 1971-72 recession; got the whole programme off to a less aggressive start; and demonstrated that the purpose of our policy was directed not against the unions but against rising prices.[1]

'N minus 1'

So in the autumn of 1970, we in the Treasury had to cobble together a makeshift policy. This emerged as the 'N minus 1' policy, so nicknamed since the rough rule of thumb was that each pay settlement should be slightly less than the one before.

The first challenge to this policy came in December with the go-slow by electricity power workers. The Chancellor made a forthright speech in which he suggested that the Government had a responsibility to show that industrial blackmail does not succeed. This somewhat perturbed the more cautious colleagues but nevertheless caught the public mood. Within a few days the go-slow was called off but the final Wilberforce settlement conceded more than was necessary.

Causes of increasing trade union power

Although the increased monopoly bargaining power of the unions is regarded by many economists as one of the main causes of accelerating inflation, it is curious that there has been little academic analysis of why this power has increased over the past quarter of a century. Yet the broad reasons are not hard to find: full employment, the increased capitalisation and sophistication of modern industry, and perhaps most important the fact that since the war almost every major strike has appeared to pay off. The desire for conciliation rather than confrontation has meant that it has become accepted practice to 'split the difference'. The result is that time after time the moderates are outfaced, and the workers in the union concerned, and in every other union (and profession), come to believe that strike action is the legitimate and effective way to get more money.

---

[1] 'There are, without doubt', (as Sir Winston Churchill commented) 'some who will be inclined to think that no element of the heroic enters into these conflicts, and that political triumphs are necessarily tarnished by vulgar methods. The noise and confusion of election crowds, the cant of phrase and formula, the burrowings of rival Caucuses, fill with weariness, and even terror, persons of exquisite sensibility. It is easy for those who take no part in the public duties of citizenship under a democratic dispensation to sniff disdainfully at the methods of modern politics and to console themselves for a lack of influence upon the course of events by the indulgence of a fastidious refinement and a meticulous consistency. But it is a poor part to play.' (*Life of Lord Randolph Churchill*, Odhams Press, 1952, p. 300.)

One does not 'blame' the unions. The task of union officials is to seek higher pay for their members. If they do not use every means within the law they would be failing in their duty. Trade unions are loosely organised heterogeneous conglomerations of many thousands of members. As such they have little power. In the same way that a bar of iron gains magnetic strength only when all its molecules 'face' one way, a union gains power only when all its members are prepared to act together. Gradually over recent years an increasing proportion of union members have come to realise that it pays to strike.

It always seemed to me that, contrary to appearances, the main purpose of the 'N minus 1' policy, and later the statutory policy, was not the detailed regulation of pay and prices, nor even the imposition of legal restraints, but the staking in public of the whole authority of the Government (thereby binding the Cabinet) to the contention that strikes for 'excessive' pay increases would not be allowed to succeed. When union members were persuaded that any strike for increased pay above the prescribed limits was bound to fail, the bargaining power of the unions was reduced and it became possible to hold inflation in check.

In case my comments below should appear to suggest that I hanker after a return to some improved form of incomes policy, let me make it clear that I do not believe that option is open. The action now re-quired is more radical.

For some time the firm implementation of the 'N minus 1' policy, supported by voluntary prices restraint by the CBI, achieved steady success. By early 1972 the annual rise in earnings was down to under 10 per cent and the annual rise in prices down to about 6 per cent. Some attribute this happy result to the lagged effect of the 1968-70 monetary squeeze, and to the rise in unemployment. It did, however, take a great deal of determination to enforce the 'N minus 1' policy and we did not get the impression that we were pushing an already closing door. Indeed the door was about to be burst open.

First miners' strike

In the spring of 1972 came the first miners' strike. It coincided with the peak of post-war unemployment. It is hard to see how its outcome can be attributed to lax monetary policy, nor how it could have been altered to a tougher monetary policy.

At the time (in the way in the real world economics are always intertwined with politics) the attention of the Cabinet was distracted by violence in Ulster and the decision to impose direct rule. The handling of the strike was left almost entirely to the National Coal Board. Government public relations *vis à vis* the miners were almost non-existent and the official stance (far from confrontation) was to say nothing and do nothing in the hope that if not provoked the miners would see reason. Not surprisingly the miners were able to build up considerable public sympathy, and when the crunch suddenly came and the lights went out, there was no alternative but to capitulate.

At the time many of those in positions of influence looked into the abyss and saw only a few days away the possibility of the country being plunged into a state of chaos not so very far removed from that which might prevail after a minor nuclear attack. If that sounds melodramatic I need only say that – with the prospect of the breakdown of power supplies, food supplies, sewerage, communications, effective government and law and order – it was the analogy that was being used at the time. That is the power that exists to hold the country to ransom: it was fear of that abyss which had an important effect on subsequent policy.

The miners' victory was followed by the successful railway strike in May. Apart from the unfortunate attempt to use the Industrial Relations Act ballot procedure where predictably a majority of those on strike would vote to continue on strike, the strike showed that (in the absence of any statutory limits) the Government could not plunge the nation into chaos (again) for the difference between an offer of 12 per cent and a claim for 13 per cent. In economic terms the railway settlement was less important than that of the miners, but it was equally humiliating for the Government. It clearly signalled the end of 'N minus 1', and of the attempt to make a free market economy work without inflation – in the absence of any restrictions on union power.

VI. Return to Incomes Policy

A new policy had to be found. Although almost all Conservative Ministers detested it as much as their subsequent critics, it was clear that, if an avalanche of accelerating pay settlements was to be avoided, there was no alternative but to revert to some form of incomes policy.[1]

Stages I, II and III

The tripartite talks in the autumn of 1972, far from confrontation, offered the unions almost all they could wish – apart from converting the Conservative Government into a Socialist administration. When this attempt at a voluntary incomes policy failed (and when the electricity power workers had conveniently been allowed their pay increase), the statutory policy was introduced, with a five-months 'freeze' as Stage I.[2] This, and Stage II (which took us to the autumn of 1973) were not seriously challenged by the unions because the new policy had overwhelming public support. It is important to remember that, despite their vaunted strength, the unions (except perhaps the miners) are not prepared to stand out against public opinion.

But public opinion is not well organised. During the tripartite talks and subsequent negotiations it became clear to me that one of the problems was that the TUC and the CBI – whatever their other differences – were both ultimately content to acquiesce in higher prices. Consumers and all those who so desperately wanted price stability had

---

[1] For the recognition that 'the Government must govern' is as much a part of traditional Tory philosophy as economic liberalism see Professor Maurice Peston, 'Conservative Economic Policy and Philosophy', *Political Quarterly*, Oct.-Dec. 1973.

[2] The statutory incomes policy was set out in the White Papers Cmnd. 5125, November 1972, Cmnd. 5205, January 1973, and Cmnd. 5444, October 1973.

no voice and no bargaining strength. The Government had to attempt the impossible dual task of trying to represent their interest as well as acting as impartial chairman.

Instead of using the Stage I standstill as a clean break with the past, the decision was taken to revert in Stage II virtually to the previous going rate of inflation. Before the miners' strike the level of pay settlements had been got down to under 10 per cent. Instead of using Stages I and II to fix pay at a level of around 3 per cent which might have been consistent with price stability, the norm was fixed at about 8 per cent.

This approach was repeated in Stage III where the pay norms (plus thresholds) were again set at a level that it was thought the unions would find acceptable even although this meant a considerable rise in the price level. In my view it would have been politically wiser to have aimed at a more or less stable price level and set tougher pay norms. Such a policy might have been challenged earlier by the unions, but the Government would have retained more public support and might therefore have stood a better chance of prevailing.

People in public life should never seek to excuse failure on the ground of bad luck – but the statutory policy had more than full measure. The phenomenal rise in world prices started just about the time the statutory policy was introduced and began to ease in the spring of 1974 as the policy came to an end. The rise in import prices plus the effect of previous pay settlements and the high Stage II and III norms all conspired to push up the cost of living. The impression was created that the policy was tough on pay and weak on prices. By the end of 1973 the polls showed it had the support of less than 50 per cent of the public.

Second miners' strike
So once again the miners went on strike. It is sometimes seriously asked why the Government picked on the miners. Under a statutory policy the Government cannot pick on anyone: once the limits are fixed, it is up to the unions which one challenges the policy. Indeed the Stage III limits were deliberately stretched as far as possible in the miners' favour. It is also asked why the Government did not settle at a reasonable compromise at an early stage: all the evidence was that the NUM would accept nothing less than their full claim; if the Government had paid up in full at the first strike threat the statutory policy would have lost all credibility.

It is not necessary to explore here how much subversive influence there was in the NUM. Suffice to say the miners were determined to get their pound of flesh; they knew from their success in 1972 that they had the power to get it. Indeed the pound of flesh was virtually conceded before the election began by the promise to backdate the implementation of the Relativity Board report. The Conservative Government had no answer to the problem of the new over-mighty subject.

The statutory policy was in a way all bluff. On the pay side the law was never invoked. Indeed because the Government had realised that all hell would break loose if any trade unionist was fined or imprisoned, the law was so constructed that in normal circumstances it was not actually illegal to strike. What the policy really meant was that the Government staked its whole reputation, its whole authority, indeed the authority of Parliament, in the hope that the unions and their members would accept 'the law' or anyway believe that the Government could never allow a strike to succeed. For 18 months the gamble worked; but when it failed the stakes were lost.

VII. Doom and Despair

The widespread sense of doom and despair which has pervaded the political and economic scene for the year since the miners' victory has arisen partly from the intractible nature of our economic problems – the mammoth balance-of-payments deficit, the accelerating rate of inflation and the looming possibility of a real slump with a return of mass unemployment. It is also partly due to a realisation that these problems are shared in some degree by almost all the other countries of the Western world, and that none knows the answer. But more than that: it has arisen from the realisation that none of the political parties in Britain can form a government capable of standing up to the power of organised labour.

The issue is constitutional as well as economic, and cannot be blamed solely on 'left-wing' unions. In the summer of 1974 the Labour Government ignominiously had to capitulate to the demands of the Ulster Protestant workers for a fundamental change in the constitution of Northern Ireland. The same tactics have been used by the nurses and hospital consultants over the political issue of pay beds. Indeed the 'social contract' itself can be regarded as the imposition of political demands by the unions.

Hyper-inflation leads to authoritarianism
The sense of doom is reinforced by the fear that inflation could so easily get out of hand. In so many other countries that has led to the end of democracy and the introduction of some form of authoritarian régime of left or right. There are signs that the structure of civilised society is beginning to crumble. Money depreciates, hoarding is endemic, shortages multiply, public services deteriorate, respect for the

law declines as more and more groups come to feel that a display of strength is the way to get what they want.

It is important to realise that it is only the fear of the large-scale strike which renders governments impotent to stop inflation. If it were not for the strike threat, a pay and prices freeze could be imposed, followed by a régime of strict monetary policy which, in a free competitive market, could be expected to produce price stability without excessive unemployment. Given price stability, interest rates would come down, exports would rise, sterling would strengthen, savings would revive, taxes could be cut, business confidence would return and fears of a slump vanish like a bad dream.

The unfaced issue

Yet even if we go on as we are, the issue of how a democratic government will resist a major strike will still have to be faced – perhaps by the present Labour Government. Even if the 'social contract' – leaky as it is – prevents the dam breaking this wage round, it is difficult to see how enough *new* political concessions to the unions can be found to secure its renewal. Equally, while it is right that the Conservative Party under its new Leader should seek a new exegesis of its traditional philosophy, it must be recognised that the Party will not become a credible alternative Government until it can suggest a method of dealing with excessive pay claims and the threat of major strikes.

The flimsy social contract is all that prevents disaster overwhelming us but it is not a long-term solution. It is a pause, a truce, in the search for the answer to the question which was posed but left unanswered in the February 1974 election – who is to govern Britain: Parliament or the unions?

VIII. New Ideals

For the past quarter of a century we have been hunting the snark of economic growth. Over the next few years almost all the growth that is achieved will be needed to pay off our overseas deficit. The standard of living is unlikely to rise.[1] North Sea oil will bring new wealth, but by the time it arrives it may well have been mortgaged in advance.

Even the advantages of economic growth are now open to question. During the past five years there has been a spate of warnings from the environmentalists that if the world continues indefinitely (or, worse, exponentially) with economic growth and population growth, then in due course the available raw materials will be exhausted, pollution of air and water will be dangerously increased, much wild life exterminated and much natural beauty destroyed. The two main reports in recent years, the *Blueprint for Survival*, and the *Limits to Growth* report,[2] were in many respects naive but they were supported by far too many eminent scientists to be ignored. Even in purely economic terms, the benefits of growth have also been called in question. In his debate with Professor Wilfred Beckerman, Dr E. J. Mishan[3] argued that it is relative, not absolute, living standards that matter. This is confirmed by

---

[1] Despite the optimistic assumptions of the recent *Public Expenditure* White Paper and the *Review* by the Cambridge Economic Policy Group, Department of Applied Economics, Cambridge, February 1975.

[2] *Blueprint for Survival*, The Ecologist, 1972; Dennis L. Meadows and others, *The Limits to Growth*, Report for the Club of Rome, 1972.

[3] The elegant debate between Professor Beckerman and Dr Mishan is to be found in the *Lloyds Bank Review*, October 1971 and October 1972; see also E. J. Mishan, *The Costs of Economic Growth*, Staples Press, 1967.

my subjective impression gained by observing the British economy over the past decade: that questions of differentials, of pay comparability between different occupations, of the 'fairness' of tax reductions, cause stronger feeling than straight changes in real take-home pay. The more Dr Mishan is right, the less will economic growth do to improve happiness or contentment. After all, perhaps the snark *was* a boojum.

Growth has been one of the main aims of the political parties, and the *raison d'être* of many policies. We have 'sought it with thimbles, and sought it with care, we have threatened its life with a railway share',[1] we have sought it with Neddy, with tax reform, with local government reform, with Royal awards and with training boards. But it must now be recognised that, even if economic growth is still desirable, it is no longer a viable political aim – in the sense that it can no longer be a central theme with which to inspire the nation.

From growth to stability

The need now is for economists, politicians, governments to concentrate with all their power on creating stability – price stability and social stability. Only thus can the free economy, the free democratic system, perhaps even Western civilisation itself, survive.

The pace of change, it is commonly observed, is accelerating. Familiar landmarks of daily life vanish with increasing rapidity. If man is no more than the product of evolution, and modern man little different in body or brain from prehistoric man, one must ask whether there is a limit to the pace of change that can be tolerated. If mankind is to exist for another 1,000 or 10,000 years one must question whether it is desirable that progress should go on gathering speed indefinitely.

We must now realise that social stability is more important than economic or technical progress: that, as a former Prime Minister, Arthur Balfour, warned in 1905,

'Society may go back as well as forward, and it has always required the constant effort, and the best elements in every society, not merely to improve it, but to maintain it at its level'.[2]

Broad national support

Some fundamental proposals aimed at preserving economic (and there-

---

[1] Lewis Carroll, *The Hunting of the Snark*.
[2] Speech at Queen's Hall, London.

fore political) freedom and restoring stability are left to the end of this Paper so that they may be set in the proper context. Since they must involve some curb on the power of the unions they could be implemented only by a government which commanded broad national support. As the 1970-74 experience proved, fundamental reforms are unlikely to succeed if they are supported only by a minority of the public. During the past year there have been many suggestions that the country has now reached a situation in which it can be effectively governed only by some form of coalition which gets away from the divisive antagonism of party politics. But there has been no very clear view as to what a coalition should do. An amorphous, lowest-common-factor administration could not carry through the radical reforms which are needed.

What is required is a government with a precise programme: tough on those who attempt to disrupt society by force and yet showing sympathy for the ideals of those, many of them in the unions, who are dissatisfied with the structure of society. It could effectively demonstrate its concern about the soul-destroying monotony of many jobs; about the appallingly offhand way in which many employers still treat their men;[1] about the way the constant emphasis on economic growth has helped to create a discontented and jealous streak in society; about the way the emphasis on efficiency has led to excessive size in many units of industry, local government and education; about the mounting feeling of frustration and loss of identity caused by over-population and over-crowding;[2] and about all the questioning of the ethics of the capitalist system which has been troubling the younger generation since the writings of Herbert Marcuse.[3] It could show it understood those who feel that the present structure of pay differentials is totally out of

---

[1] For the need to give workers a sense of involvement in industrial decision-making, Stephen Abbott, *Employee Participation*, Old Queen Street Paper, September 1973.

[2] Almost as many words were written about population as children were born during World Population Year 1974, but for a short factual article, Professor Bernard Benjamin, 'Advantages of a Smaller Population', *The Times*, 16 August, 1974. For the adverse effects of over-crowding, Robert Ardrey, *The Social Contract*, Collins, 1970.

[3] *The One Dimensional Man*, and *Eros and Society*. Also Charles Reich, *The Greening of America*, 1970. Much the same was said, more concisely, by Disraeli: '... the European talks of progress, because by an ingenious application of some scientific acquirements he has established a society which has mistaken comfort for civilisation'. (*Moneypenny and Buckle*, p. 765.)

date, and based on an age now past when there were many willing to do the dirty, dangerous jobs but few who had the education or inclination to take responsibility. It could make it clear that a free market should be allowed to establish a new pattern of differentials.[1] It could think in terms of new legislation to recognise that these days it would make better sense sometimes to organise companies or public corporations on a syndicalist basis with the workers taking the risks and the rewards, and the providers of capital taking a fixed return. All of this could be supported by politicians of all parties without harm to their traditional philosophies.

Plan for posterity

Any government which seeks to impose tough and drastic measures must first give the nation an ideal towards which to strive. 'Where there is no vision, the people perish'. One of the penalties of the race for growth and of the rapid pace of change is that there has been a constant pressure to live for the present. Yet the desire of parents to create a better life for their children is one of the strongest of human ideals.

How welcome it would be if the political sights could be lifted from the search for present prosperity to securing and improving our civilisation for future generations. Foremost that must mean having the courage to find a long-term solution to our present problems, but there are many other ways in which the quality of civilisation could be raised. There are opportunities for harnessing the immense enthusiasm for improving the environment; for raising standards of architecture; for attending to the content and quality of education – seeking wisdom instead of wealth; perhaps even for reducing the pressure on our overcrowded island by welcoming the current decline in the birth rate and bringing about a gradual reduction in the population; in short, more emphasis on stability and continuity, on the spaciousness and diversity and beauty of life, and less on size, speed, efficiency, production and technology.

---

[1] There is a paradox here. Although trade unions push up rates of pay and so help to cause inflation, the rises tend to become generalised, thus maintaining differentials. If coal-miners had no union they might by now have found their real pay improved as fast as that of the shorthand typists.

IX. New Policies

Experience of economic policy during the past five years teaches that while a stringent monetary policy and a firm control of public expenditure are essential if inflation is to be controlled, neither is sufficient. The monopoly power of the unions – or more accurately the power of the strike weapon – has made it impossible for any government to maintain either price stability or full employment, or indeed to govern in the interests of the whole nation.

The time has therefore come for all who care about the survival of freedom – economic freedom or freedom in general – and about the survival of Parliamentary democracy, calmly and rationally to start discussing the subject which has hitherto been taboo but which may become the crucial issue of this decade: whether the nation should clearly express the view that certain types of strike are anti-social and reprehensible; and to do so explicitly by putting some limitation on the so-called 'right' to strike.

It must remain an ultimate freedom for any individual to work or not to work; but this cannot give an unlimited right to organise concerted action to damage the remainder of the community. There is a long tradition of legislation to prevent monopoly exploitation. If some limitation were placed on strike action, the balance of bargaining power could be returned to equilibrium. In conjunction with a strict monetary policy, this would make possible a return to free wage bargaining and the free play of the market economy.

Emergency action
But first it is clear that emergency action must be taken to stop inflation and restore confidence in the currency. A total freeze should be imposed on both pay and prices. It may be desirable at the same time to

reconstruct the currency (as de Gaulle did to the French franc). The freeze should be kept in force until long-term measures can be implemented to preserve price stability. Of course a freeze causes injustices and rigidities but the damage would be far less than would result from accelerating inflation.

In order that the freeze on prices is not rendered ineffective or overharsh, one month could be allowed to elapse in which firms and public corporations were permitted to raise their prices to cover any past cost increases.

The slate could be wiped clean by the removal of all existing subsidies. After that, if world prices rise, some subsidies could be re-introduced. But with luck world prices will remain steady or even come down.

The result would be stability or even perhaps a gradual fall in the cost of living. Those who dismiss such a hope as fantasy are just those who a couple of years ago would have laughed at anyone who had predicted the fall in share and property values.

There is reason to hope that a freeze would not be destroyed by another miners' strike, or by a strike by another equally powerful union. Both the last two freezes, those of 1966 and 1972, were not challenged, although it is true they lasted for less than a year. A freeze represents rough justice and does not raise any questions of relative merits. It is far easier to hold a line on nil than to argue that 16 per cent is permissible but 18 per cent disastrous. Most important, the practical achievement of price stability would provide the Government with a growing popularity. If the freeze were challenged, the Government would have to stand and fight.

A freeze, however, can only be a temporary expedient. The option of following it with a statutory incomes policy is, as Mr Harold Wilson has rightly pointed out, no longer available. The unions would not comply: the bluff has been called. Nor is the control of pay and prices a viable permanent policy. Whatever adjustments, such as Relativity Boards, are introduced it is bound to be inflexible; and it would be hard even for the most enthusiastic supporter of the recent statutory policy to envisage an endless succession of Stages IV, V, VI, VII . . . stretching out year by year into the 21st century!

A similar objection applies to the many ingenious proposals for indexation, and for the taxation of excessive pay and price increases. All ultimately depend on trade union compliance. All are only shortterm expedients.

The right to strike

The only long-term solution is to limit the right to strike. This 'right' was gained as a result of the 1871 Trade Union Act, which roughly speaking made unions legal and no longer a conspiracy in restraint of trade, various other Acts passed in the 1870s, and the 1906 Trade Disputes Act, which gave any group of workers involved in a trade dispute special legal immunities. The repeal of the Industrial Relations Act brought the legal situation back to the 1906 position, and the current Government Bill extends the immunities (unique in any society anywhere) even further.

The world has changed since 1906 but many of the old attitudes gained on the hard road from Tolpuddle to Taff Vale remain: the belief that strikes are the chief protection of ill-paid and exploited workers, that they are an essential means of redistributing resources in a harsh capitalist society. Yet the statistics show that over the years the share of wages in the national income has remained virtually unchanged. Protection for the weak and low paid can be provided better by full employment and by the market. At the beginning of the century unions were weak and poor, and strikes directed primarily against individual employers. Today unions are strong, the families of strikers are eligible for social benefits, and few employers can stand the cost of resisting a strike. Often the industrial action occurs in the public corporations and is openly designed to cause inconvenience and hardship to the public – even the risk of death to the old or weak – in the (correct) belief that all this will put pressure on the Government to authorise a favourable settlement. It may sound emotive to draw a comparison with other undesirable practices such as demanding money with menaces, holding to ransom or hi-jacking. All such practices are of course illegal, but since 1906 it has been lawful to act in a similar way in a 'trade dispute' even if the victim is the whole nation.

It would not be impossible to devise an amendment to the law to outlaw strikes against the community (or strikes which exploit monopoly power). Strikes against the rule of Parliament could also be outlawed, as indeed they were from 1927 to 1946.

Any such reform would mean that official or unofficial leaders of strikes against the community would become liable to civil or criminal actions, and some would inevitably end up in jail. Any government which attempted to introduce, or thereafter to implement, legislation on these lines would face total trade union hostility and the probability of an all-out general strike.

Even if we go on as we are, at some stage some government will have to take a stand against accelerating inflation. We may, even on present prospects, face another major strike almost as serious as a general strike. Yet, as we have seen from recent experience, public sympathy is inevitably divided on any issue of pay. There might be more chance of success if the stand were taken on the real constitutional issue.

Success will only be achieved by a government which commands, and is seen to command, broad public support. This may mean some form of coalition; and the advantages of all-Party support – if it were obtainable – are obvious. But certainly if the issue is to be faced, all other political aims must be subordinated to the task of winning the support of the people. That is why it is essential to provide new ideals that can inspire not only one party but the whole nation.

Would legal reform work?
It may be asked why, if the present inflation is caused by the unions using their power against government and the law, any solution merely prescribing a change in the law is likely to work. Of course, if it were imposed by an unloved government on an unwilling people it would not. The law is only the embodiment of the will of society. If the people overwhelmingly make it clear that they consider strikes against the community reprehensible – and it may be that some time must elapse before that becomes generally accepted – the law will be obeyed. In future years everyone will wonder why it was not always so.

In present circumstances many people may find it hard to envisage a free economic system functioning without major strikes. So also before 1846 many could not imagine Britain without protection from imported food. So also before the American Civil War, there were many in the Southern States who could not imagine their economy functioning without slavery.

CONCLUSION
This Paper has been an attempt to draw conclusions from the experience of seeing economic policy from the inside during the past five years. Perhaps the most searing experience was the realisation both during the 1972 and 1974 miners' strikes that all or almost all Cabinet

Ministers (and I am sure it would be equally true of the present Government) and all or almost all senior civil servants believed that the nation could not survive an all-out general strike or even a total electricity stoppage without total chaos, large numbers of deaths in hospitals, deaths of old people, and deaths from epidemics as the sewers overflowed, hunger, starvation and riots. There was, therefore, in the last resort, *no alternative but appeasement and surrender*.

Yet now we are playing for high political stakes. If the cost of continued appeasement is accelerating inflation, mass unemployment and the collapse of democracy, there will be anarchy or revolution and just as much hardship and death in the end – if not more. In the end, as in other countries which succumb to totalitarian régimes, order will be restored – and strikes outlawed – by the terror of the secret police and the law of the machine gun.

I believe that, if need be, the nation could survive a general strike. There are still great reserves of patriotism and resourcefulness to be called upon. The disruption and damage might be as bad as that we experienced during the 1939-45 War, but few doubt that war was worth fighting for the sake of freedom. If the necessary preparations are made calmly, competently, and without fear, the chances are that the crunch would never come.

To attempt to limit the power of the new over-mighty subjects might well bring the nation to the verge of civil war. But at some stage Parliament will have to exert itself – or cease to exist. If its cause is that of democracy, freedom and stability, it will find, to its surprise, that it has almost the whole nation on its side.

IEA PUBLICATIONS

Subscription Service

An annual subscription to the IEA ensures that all regular publications are sent without further charge immediately on publication – representing a substantial saving.

The cost (including postage) is £10.00 for twelve months (£9.50 if by Banker's Order) – £7.50 for teachers and students; US $25 or equivalent for overseas subscriptions.

To: The Treasurer,
Institute of Economic Affairs,
2 Lord North Street,
Westminster,
London SW1P 3LB

Please register a subscription of £10.00 (£7.50 for teachers and bona fide students) for the twelve months beginning............................

☐ Remittance enclosed   ☐ Please send invoice

☐ I should prefer to pay by Banker's Order which reduces the subscription to £9.50.

Name...

Address...

....

Position...

Signed...

Date...

HOBART PAPERS in print

For further information about IEA publications and details of subscription services, please write to:

THE INSTITUTE OF ECONOMIC AFFAIRS
2 Lord North Street, Westminster, London SW1P 3LB